Real Estate Gift

Real Estate Gift

*How Your Church Can Acquire Major Gifts
Without Badgering Donors*

JAMES B. WOOTTON

American Charter LLC
Columbus, Ohio

First Edition, Second Printing

Wootton, James B., 1946-

    Real estate gift : how your church can acquire major gifts without badgering donors / James B. Wootton. -- 1st ed. -- Columbus, Ohio : American Charter, 2006.

    p. ; cm.
    ISBN: 978-0-9769445-0-8 (pbk.)
    Includes glossary.
    Includes bibliographical references and index.

    1. Church fund raising—Handbooks, manuals, etc. 2. Church finance—Handbooks, manuals, etc. 3. Fund raising—Handbooks, manuals, etc. 4. Nonprofit organizations—Finance—Handbooks, manuals, etc. 5. Real property, Exchange of—United States—Handbooks, manuals, etc. 6. Gifts—Taxation—United States—Handbooks, manuals, etc. I. Title.

BV772.5 .W66 2006   2005909462
254.8/.0068/1—dc22   0601

Printed and bound in the United States of America
10 9 8 7 6 5 4 3 2

Editor: David J. Glunt
Interior design: www.tothepointsolutions.com

To my wife, Diane McKean Wootton,
whose love, devotion, and patience has made
this book possible; and to our son, Matthew.

Contents

Preface . . . .*xi*

Acknowledgments . . . .*xv*

PART ONE — *In The Trenches*

Chapter 1   **Church District Headquarters** 3
How one church district headquarters
obtained a Class A office building with the
help of a major gift of a partial real estate transaction.

Chapter 2   **Adaptive Re-use: Church in a**
Shopping Center 9
Being creative on finding a workable location.

Chapter 3   **Rezoning Once, Twice, Three Times!** 17
How one property was rezoned and sold three
times by different sellers, each with large
surpluses.

Chapter 4   **Three-Legged Exchange** 23
Brokers buy first property to make a complex
exchange work.

PART TWO — *How to Acquire Your*
Real Estate Gift by Bargain Sale

Chapter 5   **Bargain Sale** 35
One broker's first hands-on experience in
doing the bargain sale.

Chapter 6   **Wonder-Working Power** 41
How little churches became big churches in an
urban environment.

Chapter 7   **How to Get a $250,000 Donation** 49
Four bargain-sale strategies: Stretch your
church's resources. Have more cash for more
ministry. Use proper leverage. Cash out the gift
and repeat.

Chapter 8   **Charitable Gift Annuities** 59
How to accommodate the donor who needs a
lifetime stream of income.

PART THREE — *Operations*

Chapter 9   **How to Ask for the Gift** 83
Identifying and cultivating donors.

Chapter 10   **Nuts and Bolts** .91
Making the offer, how much to pay, and the
mandatory donative intent.

Chapter 11   **Taxing Matters** .97
How and why to establish a for-profit
subsidiary to own and operate your major
income properties.

PART FOUR — *Income-Producing Gift Property*

Chapter 12   **Value: A Primer on Net
Operating Income** 111
How to arrive at value for income-
producing property.

Chapter 13   **Property Due Diligence** 117
Check it out: Legal, environmental,
physical inspections, and appraisals.

Afterword 125

Appendix A **IRS Forms 8282 and 8283** 127

Appendix B **Treasury Regulations** 131

Appendix C **IRS Life Expectancy Table** 133

Glossary 135

Suggested Reading 141

Bibliography 143

Resources 145

Index 147

About the Author 149

You have planted much, but have harvested little.
You eat, but never have enough. You drink, but never
have your fill. You put on clothes, but are not warm. You
earn wages, only to put them in a purse with holes in it.
This is what the Lord Almighty says: "Give careful
thought to your ways. Go up into the mountains and
bring down timber and build the house, so that I may
take pleasure in it and be honored," says the Lord.

Haggai 1:6-8 (NIV)

Preface

ON A THURSDAY MORNING IN THE SPRING OF 1980 AT
the Franklin County Courthouse in Columbus, Ohio, I
bought several properties at the auditor's auction for unpaid
taxes. I did not have sufficient capital to make all the investments on my own, but I had the backing of an investor, Ethan
Wallace, in order to bid on as many as a dozen properties
being offered. Ethan and his wife owned a nearby main street
retail business. He was an "on-fire" Christian—a sparkplug
who had organized over a dozen Christian men's groups
throughout Ohio. Included in that batch of successful bids
was a vacant lot on High Street in Columbus, which cost
$900.

The following year, after an unsuccessful period trying to
sell that property, I was driving down High Street. Looking at
the site I said, "Lord, what do you want me to do with this lot?
Nobody seems to want it." Then I glanced to the right. A sign
on the next building read "High Street Community Church."
The thought came to me, "This church could use the lot."
Then another thought, "They do not want that vacant lot."
And then I thought: "No, that thought might be from the
Lord, and I am going to find out." So I made four right turns,

went around the building, parked in front, and knocked on the front door of the church.

When the Pastor came to the door, I introduced myself. After we got acquainted, I asked, "What are you folks doing for parking?" He said: "We don't have any off-street parking. We have to park at the meters on the street, and it is a problem." I said: "Well, I feel the Lord may be leading me to donate this land to you."

To learn what the tax savings for donating the land might be, I decided to do comparable land research in the county map room at the courthouse. While I was doing the research, I saw that there was another rectangular lot adjacent to mine. I realized that if this lot were combined with mine, it would make the parking turnaround for the church much easier. The idea came to me: "Maybe I should ask the adjacent owner, a Mr. Spencer, to donate his lot to the church as well". Then conflicting thoughts: "How silly can you be? This man doesn't even know you. Living way out in the suburbs, he probably doesn't care about this church on High Street, don't make a fool of yourself."

Disregarding these misgivings, I drove to Mr. Spencer's home and knocked on his door. The full conversation took about three minutes. I told him that Ethan and I were going to donate the vacant lot to the church next door because they needed parking. If he could donate his along with ours, there might be some tax savings for him. He interrupted me and said: "OK, just do it." My heart leaped. My words stumbled out, "Mr. Wallace is planning to get an appraisal to document the tax savings." Mr. Spencer responded, "Tell him I'll pay for half of the appraisal fee." My feet barely hit the ground as I went back to the car. As I drove away, I was having my own praise service in the car. At that moment, I promised God that if He would continue showing me the way, I would make an effort to put more real estate into the hands of churches. After we completed both of the transfers, the church held a dedication service at 2:00 o'clock on a Sunday afternoon, led by the local pastor. It was an inspiring occasion for Ethan Wallace and me. Ethan went to the podium and delighted the crowd with his personal testimony and his encouragement.

With that seemingly inconsequential but joyous start, I resolved to make myself available to work on church property transactions and began my journey working toward a far greater goal. In telling these stories my intent is to help you think about possibilities you may not have considered and to give God the glory for all good things.

Acknowledgments

THIS BOOK GREW FROM THE NOTES I PREPARED FOR MY talk to a monthly "Kingdom Builder" breakfast group at New Life Church in Gahanna, Ohio. I am grateful to Don Cordle and Jim Strong, FCBA, church business administrator, for inviting me to be a guest speaker. I owe a deep debt of gratitude to my great friend Jon Hanson, author of *Good Debt, Bad Debt* (Penguin-Portfolio 2005), who not only shared with me his store of knowledge about the craft of writing and publishing but offered his encouragement throughout the writing process, at many meetings over a cup of coffee.

Thanks to my many clients and customers for the contributions they have made to this work. Without their faith in the process I would not have been challenged to dig so diligently for workable solutions. Also I would not have had the motivation or privilege to try these strategies and document the outcome.

I wish to express a special thanks to my editor, David J. Glunt, whose editorial suggestions showed remarkable sensitivity and depth of knowledge. I appreciate the professional interior design work by Mary Jo Zazueta, and for her patience in offering several excellent choices of design. I also wish to acknowledge those individuals, organizations and companies who served to offer ideas and information, and who reviewed copies of the book.

Thanks also to my wife, Diane McKean Wootton, for lending moral support throughout the process of writing and publishing.

Real Estate Gift grew out of many people's experiences before my own. Many thanks to all of you who blazed the trails that made my journey easier.

Real Estate Gift

PART ONE

In the Trenches

~

Do all the good you can,

By all the means you can,

In all the ways you can,

In all the places you can,

At all the times you can,

To all the people you can,

as long as ever you can.

— John Wesley, English theologian
and evangelist, founder of Methodism
(1703-1791)

Chapter 1

CHURCH DISTRICT HEADQUARTERS

MONEY MAY NOT GROW ON TREES, BUT YOU CAN FIND it in some pretty unusual places. Knowing where to look is the key. In real estate, the key to flexibility in transactions is equity; large amounts of equity. There is a saying in real estate exchange circles that you really have nothing with which to transact except your equity. It certainly applies in the field of charitable giving. Fortunately, in the transaction described below there was plenty of equity.

In late 2005, three top executive officers of a midwest district for a large denomination, together with their administrative assistant and I, met with the owner of a $6 million class A office building near a busy suburban interstate freeway exit.

We had been discussing and negotiating since the spring of 2005 to acquire the building for the church organization head-quarters. The transaction would be accomplished under a partial gift arrangement in which the owner would donate $750,000 as a charitable donation toward the acquisition cost, under the bargain sale rules of the Internal Revenue Code.

Over the past few years, the church leadership had become aware that their old district office facility was overdue to be replaced. With encouragement from former district leaders as well as their current governing bodies, the district officers had been actively pursuing various leads on available office space for more than a year.

One hurdle was the sale of the old office facility. The previous week the church district had listed the old facility for sale with my real estate firm. The next morning I had a breakfast meeting with one of Ohio's most prominent real estate exchange instructors, Realtor Furman Tinon. We both had been members the Columbus Real Estate Exchangers for over 25 years. Furman and I had previously collaborated on several other large and successful transactions through the years in various municipalities and townships in Ohio. I showed him a picture and details of the older office building.

Furman selected one of his long time clients who managed over 5,000 apartments in 5 states. The client was headquartered in leased office space less than 1 mile from the subject property. By 7:30 that evening Furman obtained a full price all cash signed offer for the older building. The buyer's lease was due to expire February 28, 2006 and time was of the essence. Furman counseled him to at least try an offer for somewhat less than the full price, but the buyer was so anxious to move into the space that he did not want to take the chance that another buyer would out-bid him. Full price was offered and accepted.

Another hurdle, which is the ultimate topic of this book, is how to use part of the seller's equity as a gift to make up the balance of the buyer's normal down payment. This strategy, pursuant to the bargain sale rules of the Internal Revenue Code, makes possible a donation deduction for the seller of real estate owned for a least one year. I will discuss this and other bargain sale strategies more fully in chapters 7, 9, 10, and 11. After consulting with his own C.P.A. and his lawyer at length, the owner agreed to make a partial real estate gift of $750,000 to the buyer.

The impressive two-story brick office facility features over 50,000 square feet of office and meeting space with ample parking. It would be a "signature" building.

The seller would master lease back for a minimum of 3 years from the buyer all of the new building except for the space needed by the buyer to occupy, for enough rent to pay the buyer's new mortgage, covering the cost of the loan. In essence, the buyer would become the owners of a multi-million dollar building without having to spend cash for the monthly mortgage payments. The down payment would be entirely covered by the bargain sale gift from the seller plus the sale proceeds of the much smaller old building.

The new building would be located near a prominent freeway interstate exit, in the midst of unprecedented retail, office, and traffic development, within a few blocks of scores of stores, many restaurants, and motels—most less than 15 years old. The building is first class, with an elevator, and is handicapped-accessible. These attractions would provide a very desirable destination for hundreds of church credential holders and their families across their district when they visit the district headquarters.

One of the seller's tenants had a long-term lease in the 10,000 square feet of space in the new building which the church headquarters would occupy. To make the transaction work, the seller would be willing to move the tenant to another office facility, which he owned in a nearby business park. They needed T-1 phone lines, which, with all the tenant build-out costs, would cost about $250,000 to extend to the location and make all installations. They would have to start immediately to make that investment, even though the closing, ideally for the buyer, would be when they got the money from the sale of the old building. Would the buyer be willing to increase their proposed $10,000 earnest money deposit to $250,000, in case there was no closing?

I said that the seller could not have a $250,000 deposit from the buyer. Maybe we could agree to an expedited closing; pull out all the stops. But how could the church headquarters organization pay $600,000 toward the closing of the new building out of the sale proceeds of the old building, when that sale was not to be concluded until about a month later? The seller offered to provide $600,000 of first mortgage financing on the old building, to bridge the gap until the closing for the old building was complete, even up to one year, if necessary. He also offered to provide temporary space for the church headquarters in his other nearby office facility, if needed, to let the church district's buyer into the old building, while the district headquarters' contractors would be finishing up the build-out of their new space. It would be contingent on negotiating a master lease satisfactory to both parties before closing. Deal. Everybody signed.

All the stops were pulled out, especially because we all knew that Christmas schedules were coming, and lots of people would be unreachable. Monday morning the buyer ordered an environmental site assessment phase1 report, a major building inspection; a survey of the property, and a title search. The seller expedited the due diligence by providing rent rolls, copies of leases and financial reports. The seller provided a preliminary draft of the master lease, which was forwarded to the corporate attorney for the church district. The attorney had several suggestions to improve the seller's master lease, which were accepted. It was a little stressful, but tremendous progress was made that first week.

After a few extensions to further clarify the terms of the master lease, and to secure the very best rate and terms for the new first mortgage loan, the transaction was closed smoothly.

The generosity of prominent property owners like the seller in this actual case makes it possible for tax exempt organizations to make a positive difference in the lives of more people.

Behold, I am coming soon! My reward is with me,
and I will give to everyone according to
what he has done.

- Revelation 22:12 (NIV)

Chapter 2

ADAPTIVE REUSE: CHURCH IN A SHOPPING CENTER

IN 2005 AN EVANGELICAL CHURCH IN A PROSPEROUS suburb on the outskirts of Columbus, Ohio had a growing school which needed to add a larger gymnasium. The church also wanted to provide for a larger sanctuary to accommodate future church growth. I approached the pastor about a nearby shopping center which had more than a dozen tenants, but one very large vacancy which formerly had been occupied by a large regional chain grocery store containing over 50,000 square feet. The shopping center was not for sale but the vacant space was advertised as available for lease.

We developed a partial gift plan for the owner, who is a major developer and philanthropist in the same community. The church would pay $7 million in cash and the $2 million remainder of the $9 million total value would be a charitable donation under the *Bargain Sale* rules of the Internal Revenue Code. The rent already being generated by all the small tenants would be sufficient to pay the monthly payments on the church's new $7 million first mortgage loan secured solely by the shopping center. The seller-donor would enjoy a $2 million dollar donation deduction, which he could write off against his ordinary income over six years, if needed. The $7 million in cash would be used to pay off the seller's old first mortgage loan balance of about $4 million and he would have plenty of cash to use for more land to develop. Since he had refinanced out beyond his original cost of development fifteen years prior, this would be a win-win situation.

However, after several months of working on this project it was determined that the zoning code in that suburb would not permit both the church and a school in the shopping center. The developer-philanthropist agreed that the church's $25,000 earnest money deposit would be returned to the church and the purchase contract was terminated.

An important lesson we learned from this endeavor is that while I may be able to arrange for "free" vacant space with this method, there still will be renovation costs. In round numbers, it seems that the donee church may expect to invest about 1/3 of the alternative "new-build" budget to get comparable space. So building out 50,000 square feet of vacant existing space may cost $1,650,000, instead of $5 million that 50,000 square feet of new space would cost to build, at say, $100 dollars per square foot. This procedure works very well for a church with a building to sell to raise cash, and then, by this method, be able to obtain worship space three times the size than otherwise would be possible.

After a few months a fresh foods type prospective tenant emerged for one half of the 50,000 square feet of vacant space in the same shopping center. I proposed to the church that they acquire the shopping center as a partial gift, just on its merits to produce a cash income for the church, and not lose out on such a large gift. They demurred.

After licking my wounds from ten months of fruitless efforts, I asked the leasing broker if the developer owned any other property similarly situated. He responded, "Yes, he has Leader Plaza inside the City of Columbus corporation limits, across town, a few miles away on the I-270 outer belt." It also was not for sale; just for lease.

This procedure works very well for a church with a building to sell to raise cash, and then, by this method, be able to obtain worship space three times the size than otherwise would be possible.

Leader Plaza had 77,000 square feet of space, of which 27,000 square feet was vacant. From my many church prospects with which I'm constantly working, one in particular seemed to be a good fit for Leader Plaza. They were in the process of selling their inner-city church near the Columbus downtown financial district, for $1.5 million, in order to find land in the suburbs upon which to build a brand-new facility. If they found land for $500,000, they would have $1 million with which to build say 10,000 square feet at $100 per square foot and have no debt. The inner-city church already had 27,000 square feet, albeit on three floors, in a very old building, including a 300-seat auditorium. So 10,000 square feet in a new building did not seem adequate. Due to the tremendous economies available, their church seemed to be an ideal candidate for the 27,000 square feet of vacant space in the suburban shopping center, Leader Plaza.

With Leader Plaza being worth $7.5 million I had in mind that the same developer should accept $5 million in cash and donate a $2.5 million dollar gift under the *Bargain Sale* rules of the Internal Revenue Code. We would arrange a new $5 million loan secured solely by a new first mortgage on Leader Plaza, for which the loan payments would be paid out of the rent from the existing tenants in the 50,000 square feet that was already leased. The 27,000 square feet remaining was more or less free, but needed just over $1 million in cash to renovate for a 600-seat sanctuary. This way the church would have 27,000 square feet of newly remodeled church space instead of only 10,000 square feet of new-build space, all for the same $1 million.

A proposal was developed to accomplish all the above, and, with some trepidation, remembering all the grief of the former project failing for lack of zoning, I took the new proposal to my old friend, the same developer-philanthropist. Being the magnanimous person that he is, and having true donative intent, he patiently agreed to yet another transaction.

There were obstacles. Zoning for the church use was

already in the Columbus city code, but there were a number of other challenges. The number of parking spaces required for a retail store was only one parking space for every 250 square feet of retail space. But in an assembly hall environment, such as a church, one parking space would be required for every 30 square feet of auditorium space. Since most of the retail businesses in the shopping center would either be not busy or even open at the time of the church's peak operating hours from 10 a.m. to noon on Sundays, it was felt that a variance could be obtained from the Columbus Board of Zoning Adjustments (BZA) to accommodate the church's larger parking requirements.

Since most of the retail businesses in the shopping center would either be not busy or even open at the time of the church's peak operating hours from 10 a.m. to noon on Sundays, it was felt that a variance could be obtained from the Columbus Board of Zoning Adjustments . . .

As soon as we had finished negotiating the purchase agreement, I checked the BZA calendar to apply for a variance on the parking spaces. We had exactly four days to complete a very complex application and have it delivered to the residences of 17 community leaders comprising the area commission for that section of Columbus. We worked fever-ishly with the architects in developing the new parking requirement language for the application, assembling all the other supporting information, and finally spending a couple of hours at the local Kinko's 24/7 copy center to get the packages delivered on time. The area commission voted to recommend approval, but when we got to the actual BZA hearing, we met with difficulty.

One BZA board member, who would have likely approved the request, had to properly recuse himself from the hearing due to a potential conflict. Then at the period of time allotted for public objections we heard from the senior pastor of an existing church nearby, who felt that since their own worship time was at 10 a.m., that traffic congestion would result, and the application should be denied. I then took the microphone to say that in the 50 plus years that I have been attending worship service about 50 plus Sundays a year, I had observed that most worshippers arrive in the final 7-10 min-utes before worship starts. Our applicant could easily schedule its time at either 9:30 a.m. or 10:30 a.m. and there would be no such traffic congestion. With our applicant pastor voicing his agreement, the zoning adjustment was approved.

Although we were not aware at the time of entering into our purchase contract, the mortgage commitment that the church would obtain required the sale of their inner city prop-erty first. This set in motion a series of domino type transactions to make this possible. Ours would be the final leg of a three-legged transaction. Transaction number one was for a condo redeveloper to buy property number one, which was the building of yet another inner city church, which would in turn purchase my client church's old building near downtown.

In the end, the second transaction happened on a Monday about one month after the condo transaction had closed, and on Wednesday, two days later, the church acquired the $7,500,000 Leader Plaza for $5,000,000 with a $2.5 million gift from the seller-philanthropist. Thanks to the diligent pursuit of this opportunity by the senior pastor; and the patience and philanthropy of this generous donor, my client church will have 27,000 square feet of newly renovated church space to reach and serve the community, instead of 10,000 square feet of new-build space. Everybody won.

"It is impossible to rightly govern a nation without God."

~ George Washington, 1st U.S. President
(1732-1799)

Chapter 3

REZONING ONCE, TWICE, THREE TIMES!

A WORTHINGTON AREA CHURCH ENGAGED ME TO ACQUIRE 10 to 15 acres for future church development within easy driving distance from the Worthington, Ohio greater community. I discovered two listings of 6 acres each, side by side, but marketed by two different brokerage firms. One of the owners was also a broker in the Columbus Real Estate Exchangers group of which I had very recently served as president. The two tracts of land were located near the new I-71 and Polaris Parkway intersection. We negotiated to buy both 6-acre tracts, each contingent on the successful acquisition of the other and closed both of them on the same day for an aggregate cost of

$230,000, including a rentable house on each of them. Five years later the church envisioned a larger opportunity and asked me to sell the 12 acres for them.

From my real estate brokerage signage, a school parent from a Christian school on the north side of Columbus phoned me to inquire about the land to see if it might be suitable for rezoning for a school. I explained to her that there would have to be rezoning hearings and due diligence performed to determine if there was adequate sewer and water capacity available for school usage. The senior pastor of the church that sponsored the school met with me. After several detailed inquiries he felt the church would be ready to start the acquisition process. Some churches have many hoops to go through, starting with a building committee established by the church board, including other key leaders in the church; then with the committee's recommendation, approval by the board itself, but contingent upon ultimate approval by the congregation at a special business meeting convened for the purpose of considering this acquisition. Sometimes, the whole matter is further contingent upon obtaining the approval and perhaps a loan guarantee from some higher governing body at a district, regional or conference level. The pastor explained to me that his church from many decades back had its roots in the Presbyterian Church and still maintained much of that church's organizational structure. Thankfully, for me as a broker, the local church was autonomous and had total sovereignty to decide on property matters at the local congregation level.

I have found from my years of church property experience that is wise to allow time not only for the minimum, usually two weeks of notification before a congregational business meeting, but also time to schedule an intervening informational meeting, so that everyone is better prepared to decide on such an important issue as the acquisition or sale of real estate. This may require allowing a total of four weeks for approval, instead of just two weeks.

The local church was autonomous and had total sovereignty to decide on property matters at the local congregation level.

This particular congregation was rather deliberate in their approach and their governing body within the local church had many questions, and required me to provide ample supporting data for their decision making process. Some of the leaders had significant real estate experience of their own, and realized some of the pitfalls of which to be wary.

An engineering firm was engaged by the new church to determine the location and the cost to extend sanitary sewer. It turned out to be about a quarter of a mile away, estimated to cost $85,000 because the there were some ups and downs in the elevation between the source and the destination. With water the depth is just 4.5 feet below grade level because the pressure comes from a water tank high above the ground. However, with sewage, it is normally moves by gravity, and it only moves one way: downhill. Therefore swales, hills and valleys often require some very deep (and wide) cuts, at great expense. Because the water line serving the property was only four inches in diameter, a sticking point emerged on how to prove to the local township fire department in Delaware County, Ohio that there would be enough water in the onsite pond to provide sufficient water volume in case of a fire at the school. The township had established a requirement that a stand-alone, private, dry fire hydrant be installed with a pipe leading down into the pond, so that in the event of a fire, the fire fighters could connect a hose to pump water from the pond.

Quasi-scientifically, we measured the depth of the pond at a dozen locations and carefully recorded the results on a hand-drawn map of the pond.

I called my friend at church, Don Bentley, and asked if I could use his boat to measure the depth of the pond. Don and his wife Doris, who were retired, were spending their winters every year providing free labor to construct new church facilities all over the country. Not only did Don provide the boat, but he delivered it and went out on the pond with me to take all the measurements. I offered to pay him, but he would not take a dime.

Quasi-scientifically, we measured the depth of the pond at a dozen locations and carefully recorded the results on a hand-drawn map of the pond. We then obtained an estimate of the water volume from an oil and gas engineer, experienced in calculating volumetrics.

After working with the zoning officials to gain approval for the school, the school's sponsoring church acquired the 12 acres for about twice the acquisition cost 5 years prior. With the profit from that closing, the selling church bought even more acreage a short distance further out in exurbia, and were thereby able to use that new land as their equity requirement to obtain a construction loan to build their first church building. What a feeling!

After a few years of weighing their options, the new owner eventually decided to build a gymnasium at their original site and this land became surplus to their requirements,

The new owner asked me to find a buyer for the land so they could use the profits toward building a gymnasium next to their existing school. I did, and it was resold for $675,000 in June 23, 1999 to a major developer.

That same developer who, on some other occasion, had been at odds with city development officials over housing density for some proposed housing project, was now in the enviable position of choosing in a bidding war of benefits to be received from the winner of two municipalities which were contending to get all the municipal income taxes that would be generated by the addition of new office workers. Today there are two large class A brick office buildings on the site. I was gaining valuable experience for more complicated deals to come.

"Never, never, never, never give up."

-Sir Winston Churchill, statesman, historian,
and biographer (1874-1965)

Chapter 4

THREE-LEGGED EXCHANGE

3-LEGGED EXCHANGE
BROKERS BUY FIRST PROPERTY
TO MAKE A COMPLEX EXCHANGE WORK
Adaptive Reuse: Converting Two
Commercial Buildings to Churches

IS IT STILL POSSIBLE TO ESTABLISH AND GROW A CHURCH
to meet the needs of people inside a fully developed city,
instead of out in suburbia? The Reverend Jim Palmer's story
shows how it was accomplished, against all odds.

Finding land for new church building is easier in the suburbs, where cornfields ripe for development beckon at
relatively low. prices, compared to scarce land in the urban
areas.

Finding land for new church building is easier in the suburbs, where
cornfields ripe for development
beckon at relatively low prices.

The Reverend Jim Palmer pastored Capital City Church,
with a mission to minister to the needs of students at The
Ohio State University campus, plus other residents within
about 5 miles north of the university. Many of his church's
core group had previously attended the campus ministry group
Chi Alpha. They were determined to find a church building
within their location parameters. In the meantime, the church
grew to about 120 in total attendance by meeting in rented
public school buildings. This meant putting up chairs, taking
down chairs, setting up and tearing down a sound system and
all the other accoutrements of ministry each and every week.
Mid-week meetings were very difficult to accommodate.

The pastor and I looked at several very expensive tracts of
land over a period of many months, before word came that the
former Bliss College Building had come on the market.

Bliss College, a business school, occupied a very well constructed brick building handsomely accented with limestone,
in the Columbus community of Clintonville, about 3 miles
north of the university campus. Clintonville is a very well
maintained residential neighborhood of homes built after
World War II, and has been home to many of the political
leaders of Columbus and Franklin County. The building that
Bliss College occupied was constructed in 1955 to be the
headquarters for Blue Cross Insurance Company.

The church decided that this building could be adapted as

their meeting place. The latest trend in preservation is adaptive reuse, the process of modifying an already existing structure by adapting it to modern needs while maintaining many elements of the structure's character and unique history. Although the building may have outlived its original function, its classic design served as a testimony to the past.

Bliss College, which was organized in 1899, acquired the property in 1970, as Blue Cross moved downtown to a much larger facility on Main Street. Bliss College was not an accredited liberal arts college but turned out thousands of students with a solid basic 2-year education in several courses of study, especially in business. After nine decades, it fell on hard times and was closed in 1993.

With three floors of 8,000 square feet each of solid classroom and office space, including one floor adaptable for an assembly hall, I believed the property could be worth as much as $840,000, with just enough improvements to make it rentable again for office space.

Pastor Palmer led the church through more than $250,000 in capital improvements, including making the building handicapped accessible, and gutting the first floor to accommodate the new sanctuary. I visited the building after 6 months and was astonished to see the results. New wallpaper, carpet, sconces, an awning, and a total repainting restored the building's look and elegant feeling beyond what it ever was with either Bliss College or Blue Cross. The congregation flourished, and after about 5 years they began to feel the need for more sanctuary space. We started looking again, while tentatively soliciting offers for the building. Any sale would necessarily have to be contingent upon obtaining suitable replacement property.

I was interested in this challenge because I had been (and still am) an active member of a group of commercial realtors specializing in tax-deferred exchanges of real estate, called Columbus Real Estate Exchangers (CREE). In 1984 I was President of that group and later went on to become President of the statewide parent organization called Ohio Commercial Realtors Exchange Association.

The most respected teacher on such exchanges in the state of Ohio is Furman Tinon, a member of CREE as well as three other exchanging organizations. He taught us years ago that when Realtors are involved in a series of exchanges, (Able trades a $100,000 property as a down payment on Baker's $300,000 property, who in turn trades his $300,000 equity as a down payment on Clark's $900,000 property) some pretty large commissions can result. The problem arises when all the transactions are contingent on finding a cash-out buyer for property number one, because neither Baker or Clark really want to keep it.

> The problem arises when all the transactions are contingent on finding a cash-out buyer for property number one, because neither Baker or Clark really want to keep it.

Furman Tinon taught us that when this happens, the solution is for the Realtors themselves to buy property number one, to trigger all the fees, which will more than pay for it. Nice theory, but what about real life?

Two brothers, Greg and Scott Hrabcak, are prominent in the CREE organization. They are both knowledgeable individuals, experienced, and successful. Scott came to me one day and asked if I still had available the church property that was meeting in the former Bliss College Building. I replied, "It is available for $1,490,000, but only if we can find suitable replacement property for the owner, which is a church." Scott had a non-profit, county-sponsored job-help organization known as COVA, an acronym for The Center of Vocational Alternatives, which wanted a building such as the former Bliss College building. But the deal could move forward only if COVA could complete the sale of their existing building at 29 East Fifth Avenue, which was on the market for $395,000. They already had an agreement with another church to buy it, contingent upon financing. There being considerable interest, we agreed to start with inspections.

Ron Lowry, a haberdasher with Tom James of Greater Columbus, was a member of Capital City Church's church board. His wife Connie was a regular customer at a commercial building on Columbus's far northwest side, less than 3 miles away, and in their desired church relocation area. She had heard that the building had previously been for sale and mentioned it to Pastor Palmer as a venue to accommodate the church's expansion. He called me to have coffee at Bob Evans in Worthington to explore the possibilities.

I remembered that Greg Hrabcak had offered the northwest commercial building at a CREE meeting approximately 2 years prior. I approached Greg and asked him if it was still available. He made a phone call and said we could have it for just under a million dollars.

After several furious rounds of intense negotiations over

several months, with various boards for all three owners meeting sporadically, all three transactions were scheduled to close, contingent on all the others being closed. Capital City church would acquire the northwest commercial building for $891,000; COVA would acquire Capital City Church's former Bliss College Building for $1,420,000; and Cova's building at 29 East Fifth Avenue would be sold for $375,000 in cash.

However, a severe problem arose. The buyer for the smallest property, 29 East Fifth Avenue, did not satisfy its contingencies. Without that sale, all transactions were dead. It was time for prayer.

I now believe God had foreknowledge of this transaction when Furman Tinon was training us years ago on the nuances of how to handle a difficult three-way closing. We had been brought together "for a time such as this." God would use Furman Tinon to help Capital City Church obtain its extremely difficult goal, and thereby touch the lives of many more hundreds for the cause of Christ. As Furman Tinon says at the conclusion of each of his own speeches: "What we are is God's gift to us, what we do for others is our gift to God." Many thanks to Furman. I trust his reward will be eternal.

The Hrabcak brothers and I huddled at their real estate office and cut an emergency deal to save the whole transaction from cratering.

The Hrabcak brothers and I huddled at their real estate office to cut an emergency deal to save the whole transaction from cratering. As an inducement to get Greg and Scott to borrow the difference and take title to 29 East Fifth Avenue, I forfeited my entire fee on the $891,000 northwest commercial building. I also deferred $25,000 of my other fees until the Hrabcaks were able to later re-sell 29 East Fifth Avenue.

We closed all three transactions on January 31, 2002, using one very large closing table and two break-out rooms. With all the clients, title officers, attorneys and brokers we had enough people in that huge conference room to hold a church service, if only someone could have come up with an offering plate!

Engaging the design/build services of The McKnight Group of Grove City, Ohio, Capital City Church then totally remodeled and expanded the northwest commercial building so that the new sanctuary could hold 350. They are still ministering to their growing urban congregation in northwest Columbus and to The Ohio State University students. Mission accomplished.

One more note: The Hrabcaks were indeed men of their word. They did re-sell 29 East Fifth Avenue before November 2002. I had much for which to be thankful on Thanksgiving Day.

"We are never defeated unless we give up on God."

—-Ronald W. Reagan, Lifeguard, athlete,
movie star, Governor, 40th U.S. President
(1911-2004)

―――――――――――――――――

"I don't want all the property in the world,
but I do want all that which borders mine."

—Texas rancher

PART TWO

*How to Acquire Your Real
Estate Gift by Bargain Sale*

❧

Chapter 5

BARGAIN SALE

Bordering Properties

EVANGEL TEMPLE ASSEMBLY OF GOD, UNDER THE LEAD-
ership of Senior Pastor Gene Speich, first acquired land in
1978 for future construction of a church and Christian school
in Gahanna. It included 12 acres, with 326 feet of frontage on
Gahanna's most important thoroughfare, at 817 North
Hamilton Road. In the 1980's the church completed several
million dollars of construction and every time a bordering
property became available they endeavored to acquire it. There
were a few challenges along the way.

When they started, the land was not served by natural gas,
nor public sewer and water. Pastor Speich personally paid for
one vacant lot in an adjacent subdivision in order to gain

access to municipal sewer and water at the next street in the subdivision. In 1980 the church invested $150,000 extra for the site work and to extend water and sewer lines to serve the first building, which was named the Family Life Center. The FLC initially accommodated Evangel Christian Academy during the weekdays and the church on Sundays. ECA included pre-school through sixth grade elementary school.

For the first six years the heating fuel was propane gas. When they added a gymnasium plus additional classrooms in a new facility called the Multi Purpose Center, they persuaded the Columbia Gas Company to extend their natural gas line about 1,500 feet to the church property. But only after Columbia Gas conducted a survey to determine how many all-electric homes in the nearby subdivisions would convert to gas if made available. After all utilities were secured, Pastor Speich sold the connecting vacant subdivision lot to the church, with no mark-up, not even for interest. It was later sold to a private home builder, but reserving an easement for the utility lines, plus yielding a tidy profit for the church.

The church bought one and one-half adjacent acres at a favorable cost from its members, Don and Doris Bentley, increasing the Hamilton Road frontage by 132 feet. Later, another bordering property owner offered the church his home on one and one-half acres adding another 132 feet. When I met with him I proposed that he would carry owner financing for the sale price with a substantial down payment from the church. He said: "Jim I can't do that because I will need the money to pay for our next home. "That's no problem," I explained. With the down payment money you will be receiving at closing, you could just borrow the rest of the money for the next home, and the money the church pays you each month together with the same rate of interest, supplies you with the funds to pay your new payment, and the net result is just the same." He did and we closed.

After a few years, the church refinanced all its property for yet another building expansion, and the seller was paid in full. It worked out perfectly, for all concerned. Now Evangel had 590 feet of frontage on a very important street. Also, the houses on the properties provided valuable staff housing and a place for an occasional visiting missionary. Septic systems for the houses acquired were replaced by connections to the church's main sewer line and electricity was upgraded. Now the rectangular shape of the original 15 acre tract had been restored and high visibility from the street was feasible.

Learning about the Bargain Sale Gift

Evangel Temple Assembly of God had acquired all the available property bordering its suburban mega church in Gahanna, Ohio, except one house to the north at 4085 N. Hamilton Road. The property was owned by Dan Abraham, a prominent attorney and long time resident of Gahanna. The little house felt cramped to Dan and his wife Susan with the arrival of their first child. Dan asked me to see if the church would be interested in it. After discussions and his consulting with his C.P.A., it was agreed that Dan Abraham would provide a $25,000 charitable donation to the church as part of a bargain sale of the property to the church. Being an attorney, he made all the arrangements and the closing on April 26, 1996 was as smooth as silk. Dan Abraham did everything he promised and more. It was indeed a pleasure doing business with him. This was a milestone for me, marking the beginning of my interest in the fascinating Bargain Sale charity model of partial real estate donations to churches.

As an aside: Evangel's road frontage was now 710 feet.

Disaster Relief Warehouse

In 2003, a well experienced pastor who was indeed a pastor's pastor, with oversight for more than 2 dozen churches in his division, referred me to provide real estate counsel to a certain pastor in his division, whom we will call Travis Duncan. Rev. Duncan, who operates a large food bank, was formerly a linebacker for a major university football team, perennially one of the top twenty five teams in the United States. He had gusto galore, and determination to make a difference in the lives of many people, right where they live. He had expanded the food bank, and was running seven semi-trucks for food and supplies where they were needed most. He desperately needed more space to operate.

The food bank was interested in acquiring a modern warehouse facility nearby, which had been listed locally for sale at $1,200,000. After I explained some of the nuances of the bargain sale real estate transaction, the local Realtor agreed to a standard co-op brokerage arrangement with me representing the non-profit buyer and with them representing the seller.

There was a stage of making the seller more familiar with the operations and background of the buyer, because donative intent is mandatory. The concept of donative intent will be explained more fully in subsequent chapters. After a few months of discussions and exploring the various possibilities, the seller in that transaction agreed to provide a $300,000 donation credit on the total value of $1,200,000, to be confirmed by an independent qualified appraisal, pursuant to the rules of the Internal Revenue Code governing partial gifts of real estate to qualified charities, such as this. The buyer came up with $200,000 of cash of its own, and therefore, came out of the closing with $500,000 of solid equity capital, making for a very viable transaction.

The $300,000 credit was a gift from the seller, under the bargain sale rules of the tax code, making the whole transaction possible. The most rewarding part of all was that it made a difference in the lives of people in need.

"Ask, and ye shall receive, that your joy may be full."

- John 16:24 (KJV)

Chapter 6

WONDER-WORKING
POWER

MARK CAMERON IS A RETIRED MINISTER, WHO SELLS REAL estate. He still accepts over 20 invitations per year as a guest speaker in churches temporarily between pastors or for one who is on vacation. Several times I visited with Mark to just talk about his experiences across the years and the marvelous things accomplished for the cause of Christ. My discussions with pastors like Mark and others across many denominations have led me to the conclusion that it's not so much the church roster upon which our name is recorded, but instead it is a personal faith in Christ's redemption for us individually that matters.

In 2001 Mark referred to me to a church property near the old Columbus Clippers Baseball Stadium, very close to the urban core. Averaging less than 30 in attendance, the congregation had decided to dispose of their church building, give all the proceeds to their missions department, and cancel their charter.

I listed for sale the church building and four lots upon which it is situated on a Tuesday, presented it to a group of commercial Realtors on Thursday, and received an offer by Saturday, from a pastor whom we will call Martin Boyd, leading a fast growing church located in rented storefront space in the inner city. We closed within 60 days, and Pastor Boyd immediately started a growth cycle, which had him looking for more space within three years. From the outset, his congrega-

> They had decided to dispose of their church building, give all the proceeds to their missions department, and cancel their charter.

tion had improved the property, painted it and made it more attractive overall. One difficulty emerging from the continued growth was the limited parking available, and some of the neighbors express their discontent due to the necessary use of on street parking in a mostly residential neighborhood.

In February 2004 I got a call from Barbara Bowen, a bank loan officer, who had been financing many of my church transactions. She suggested I call a pastor whom we will call

Lucas Tucker, who had a church building that would seat over 900. Pastor Tucker was thinking of moving to the next level.

> I listed the church property for $800,000. I showed the building to Pastor Boyd on Friday; he brought in his whole congregation to try it out on Sunday evening, and they gave us a full price offer before they left the building.

I met with Pastor Tucker at the property, and it was suggested that I list the church property for sale at $800,000. Soon after I showed the building to Pastor Boyd on a Friday; he brought in his whole congregation to try it out on a Sunday evening, and we had a full price offer from the buying church before they left the building.

The lender was more than happy to make the loan to Pastor Boyd's church since the bank already had three years of excellent payment history. But the bank did require that the buyer's own church property be sold to provide ample equity to add to their already significant cash reserves.

Pastor Boyd phoned a pastor friend, whose church was in the same denomination, but was renting space in a church building owned by a different denomination. Their congregations very soon reached an agreement, and they began make final arrangements with the same bank providing funding for all the closings. The transactions took place back to back and were smooth as silk.

> They grew as a church for Ghanaian immigrants from zero to over 400 in attendance within 12 months.

Ghanaians Meet Columbus

In 2001, Pastor Bismark Akomeah arrived from Ghana, credentialed with the Assemblies of God from their District in Ghana, in West Africa. He established his first congregation, known as Jesus Power Assembly of God, by renting space in an extra building owned by a church in northeast Columbus. Under the dynamic leadership of Pastor Bismark Akomeah, they grew as a church for Ghanaian immigrants from zero to over 400 in attendance within 12 months, and were desperate for their own space. But how could we find land to build in such a fully developed urban environment?

Again, Barbara Bowen came to the rescue. A former banking associate was now a Realtor and had an office building for sale with over 2 acres of surplus land about 2 miles north of the existing church's rented facility, and closer to the northern Columbus outer belt, I-270. We negotiated a satisfactory purchase contract with all the necessary due diligence contingencies. Mel Felty, principal in the architectural firm of Felty-Heinlen Architects and Planners, Inc., of Mansfield, Ohio, specializing in the design of religious facilities, discovered that the office building had interior bearing walls. It would cost about $150,000 to re-work the building, considering the cost of dealing with the bearing wall, new flooring to bear all the added weight of the people, and new heating and air conditioning. Mel asked, "Why not just spend about $350,000 and get a whole new additional building for the sanctuary and use the existing office building for classrooms?" That seemed to be an excellent solution. Zoning was cleared without changing the existing office zoning, but with the parking being somewhat tight. The architect designed the auditorium mathematically to fit the parking available. We closed.

They settled on a contractor who had a long established track record, and were well satisfied that the construction was completed on time and within the budget. The Ghanaian congregation is now occupying their new buildings and growing. Jesus Power Assembly of God had over 500 at their dedication service, many decked out in their authentic African dress. They worshiped, preached, prayed, and sang until 2:00 p.m.

From the first few Sundays' attendance, it was almost immediately apparent that more facilities would be needed in the future. Although it was not listed for sale, we set about to acquire the house adjacent to the north, which had a rear lot with substantial depth, providing expansion space for fifteen extra cars. The owner was willing to do something to accommodate the church, but was vitally concerned for the preservation of some of his mature trees beyond the sale date. The church's architect, Mel Felty, submitted a site plan that retained most of the biggest trees. When we finally reached an agreement, the seller agreed to finance most of the purchase price at a favorable rate of interest. Soon after that closing, two more acres adjacent to the south of the church came on the market. I negotiated a quick purchase and closing of that one for the church as well. At this juncture the Pastor Akomeah's church was well situated for future growth.

What's in a Name?

I heard a cute story about a youngster who invited his school friend to come to his church's Easter drama. "Oh! I couldn't possibly do that." his young friend replied. "Why not?" he countered. "Well, our family goes to a church of a different abomination!" he said.

> There seems to be a definite trend towards diminishing the national brand. . . . The denomination's name will be barely mentioned in very small lettering at the bottom of the sign, if at all.

From my unscientific observation, but working with dozens of churches and studying hundreds, there seems to be a definite trend towards diminishing the national brand, so to speak. Typically the name on the church sign will be something like "Monument River Community Church", in bold lettering. Sometimes the denomination's name will be barely mentioned in very small lettering at the bottom of the sign, if at all. Maybe there is a greater emphasis on Christ, and less on doctrinal differences. That seems to me to be a good thing.

"If a person gets his attitude toward money straight,
it will help straighten out almost every other area
in his life."

—Billy Graham, Evangelist. (1918-

Chapter 7

How to Get a $250,000 Donation

Bargain Sale Strategy Number 1: Stretch your resources.

A BARGAIN SALE IS PART GIFT AND PART SALE UNDER SECTION 170 of the Internal Revenue Code. The reduced price is the bargain sale price and the remainder is a gift, which must be validated by a determination of the property's fair market value by an independent, qualified appraiser.

For the sake of illustration, consider the case of a church that wants to buy a property valued at $1,000,000 from a Mr. Baker. Step one of the journey is developing the relationship with the property owner. The church representative should provide Mr. Baker with a complete update about the church, reviewing in detail its history, its current operations and its plans for the future, no matter how long (or recently) Mr. Baker has known of the church's ministry. After the relationship is well established and donative intent is perceived, the donative proposal would be presented providing for a bargain

Why would you put your congregation through the agony of an extended capital fund raising campaign, when you can reach $250,000 of the total with the swish of a pen by a generous donor?

sale price of $750,000 to be paid in cash to the seller-donor which you the church will either raise through pledges or through conventional financing, plus his gift of $250,000. The seller-donor would benefit from the tax savings generated by the $250,000 donation deduction. For the sake of this example we will say his federal income tax rate is 35%, which would yield an actual cash savings of $87,500. Adding the tax savings to the $750,000 provides $837,500 for the seller-donor. Moreover, many states allow state income tax charitable deductions that follow federal charitable deducibility guidelines, if itemized. Check with your C.P.A. first. He will have a capital gains tax to pay, equal to 15% of the difference between his adjusted basis (discussed in Chapter 10) and the bargain sale price, but he still will have a very nice total package when the seller-donor considers the following factors:

1. The immeasurable benefit his gift will be to the community;

2. Otherwise continuing the property costs: taxes, depreciation, maintenance, utilities, and insurance;

3. The opportunity cost because of what else he could be doing profitably and immediately with the funds, while waiting perhaps many months for a sale.

The reduced price is the bargain sale price and the remainder is a gift.

Considering the above bundle of benefits, the immediacy of this transaction, and most importantly, the good it will do for the community, it adds up to a very handsome package for the seller. As it has been proven, there is no need for a church to struggle for a huge down payment for its next large property purchase. Why put the congregation through the agony of an extended capital fund raising campaign, when you can reach $250,000 of the total with the swish of a pen by a generous donor.

Bargain Sale Strategy Number 2: We can use our cash better for ministry.

Consider the case of a financially healthy church in exurbia with a strong aversion to debt of any kind (for inspiration read *Good Debt Bad Debt* by Jon Hanson, Portfolio 2005). Before acquiring a $1 million property they had already raised $1 million in cash, which was drawing interest in a bank. If they made exactly the same donative proposal to Mr. Baker to pay the donor $750,000.00 of the church's cash by a using the bargain sale tool, there would be $250,000.00 extra cash remaining in the bank. This might pay for renovation, furniture, ministry programs, staff and it could fulfill the great commission by enabling missionaries to be witnesses "unto the uttermost part of the earth." (Acts 1:8 –(KJV)

Bargain Sale Strategy Number 3: Leveraged Liturgists

Here is an example of the strategy that says, "Never make another down payment for property again." This church loves leverage. They need a continuous stream of income to increase charitable programs or to pay the payments on their existing debt. They have an annual budget of $2 million including their elementary school and other charitable programs. The planned-giving officer develops a rapport with Mr. Caldwell, the owner of a shopping center, valued at $4 million. Using the shopping center as the sole collateral, the church obtains a $3 million mortgage loan from a life insurance company to pay to the seller-donor Mr. Caldwell. The remaining equity of $1 million becomes a donation deduction for Mr. Caldwell.

This bargain sale strategy leaves you owing only 75% of the property's value, and having a solid equity equal to 25% of the total property value.

Using a 10% capitalization rate the net operating income would be $400,000.00 per year. Of this, about $300,000.00

per year would be used for debt service on the $3 million loan, and $100,000.00 would be available each year for the church to use for its programs or to pay down its other debt. Someone may ask, "Isn't this just another nothing-down real estate program?" No, because those programs leave you owing 100% of the property's value and having no equity.

This bargain sale strategy leaves you owing only 75% of the property's value, and having a solid equity equal to 25% of the total property value.

A properly funded large building program should not be paid for by an over reliance on any one financing mechanism. Having a 100% bank loan could leave the church strapped financially, unable to budget for ministries and programs for many years into the future.

On the other hand, asking the congregation to completely pay in cash 100% for a large expansion over the relatively short span of say, a three year capital campaign, is very difficult for most churches. By adding the third component of a major real estate gift via any of the four bargain-sale strategies explained above, the burden will be shared among three resources, establishing a balanced funding program. Note however, that it may be necessary for the buyer to add a small component of cash towards the down payment, perhaps an additional ten percent, even if the Seller has agreed to donate 25%. Unless the lender is satisfied with the borrowers other financial resources, property, liquidity and history of growth, it may be reluctant to loan even 75%, when the buyer has absolutely nothing at stake.

Non-profit organizations need to be aware that if they borrow money to buy income producing rental property, then the Internal Revenue Code requires that the rental income be taxed, as Unrelated Business Income. The tax due is called Unrelated Business Income Tax (UBIT).

However there is an exemption from the UBIT for non-profit organizations which acquire rental income property in the neighborhood of their existing tax exempt operations, with the intention to convert the property acquired to their exempt purpose within 10 years (15 years for churches). Therefore in the above example, if the church were to acquire the above shopping center from Mr. Caldwell, and use one large vacancy (which is why Mr. Caldwell put the property on the market) for an immediate ministry, with the intention of using the entire land area for expanded ministry programs, gradually over a 15 years time span, as the other commercial tenants' leases expire, then the rental income would not be subject to UBIT even if part of the acquisition cost is borrowed, under the *neighborhood land exemption.*

Retail properties with a single large vacancy will more likely have real estate broker's signage which says "Available," not necessarily "For Lease" or "For Sale."

Retail properties with a single large vacancy will more likely have real estate broker's signage which says "Available", not necessarily "For Lease" or "For Sale." This is your invitation to start the process to obtain the bargain-sale real estate gift. The huge equity that is possible with the bargain-sale donation, in fact provides you the almost free space ready to improve for ministry, while the rental income from the remaining commercial tenants can pay for the bulk of the mortgage required to complete the purchase.

Bargain Sale Strategy Number 4: Cash out the gift, and repeat.

Perhaps your church would just like to have the $250,000 in cash. Then cash out the gift. But you will process the gift in phases. The money comes at the end. The rewards are great for both for the church and the donor. Greatly over-simplified, it works like this:

1. Develop a rapport with the seller-donor.
2. Evaluate the property and obtain a preliminary title report to estimate indebtedness.
3. Create the proposal and close the transaction to acquire the property.
4. Put the property on the market and sell it for cash. Pick up your $250,000.

By the time you re-sell it in 3 or 4 years, the property might be worth an extra 10-12%. Not on the $250,000, but the entire $1,000,000. If the property were properly selected for value from the beginning, and then it grows in value at the rate of inflation, say 3% per year. That would be about 12% in 4 years, or an extra $120,000; so you get $370,000 (less costs), not $250,000. Of course there will be some holding costs, real estate commissions and other closing costs. However, in that price range, the fees, always negotiable, are usually a lower percentage than with the sale of a typical house.

A few words of caution: Some charities have reported that properties donated by say, an alumnus who could not dump the property any other way, could only obtain 70 to 80 % of the original donation amount, as appraised by the donor's appraiser. By carefully screening acceptable donations, the goal is for that not to be the case.

The resale date cannot be specified by the donor. Any resale must be in the donee organization's sole discretion.

If the property is resold in less than 2 years, the donee organization must report the sale to IRS on Form 8282. If the resale price within 2 years is lower than the fair market appraised value originally claimed on form 8283, IRS could possibly challenge the donor's deduction that had been claimed on Form 8283. However, there must not be any agreement with the donor for the donee organization to hold the property beyond the 2 years before selling it. The resale date cannot be specified by the donor. Any resale must be in the donee organization's sole discretion.

"The measure of the morality of any society
is the shape of things it leaves to its children."

- Dietrich Bonhoeffer, Theologian, author,
central figure in the Protestant struggle
against Nazism (1906-1945)

If anyone does not provide for his relatives,
and especially for his immediate family, he has
denied the faith and is worse than an unbeliever."

- Timothy 5:8 (NIV)

Chapter 8

CHARITABLE GIFT ANNUITIES

IN THE PROCESS OF WORKING ACTIVELY IN PURSUING major gifts of real estate, you are eventually going to come across a donor who is interested in donating real estate but needs to supplement his other income in retirement years. Being a 501(C)(3) charity, the church is in an ideal position to provide an income stream for the rest of the donor's life, through a charitable gift annuity agreement that can also provide significant tax benefits, starting in the first year.

In the early stages of adulthood, a big concern for family breadwinners is that they may die too soon. But after the children are grown and retirement age approaches, a new concern develops: "What if I live too long—outlive my capital." *USA*

Today reported that more than half of Americans are worried about having enough money for retirement. Of all financial tools available, nothing quite solves that problem like an annuity, because the annuitant can never outlive the steam of income. It provides financial security when it is needed the most.

The church is the issuer of the annuity and the donor and/or spouse is the annuitant. The donor transfers the real estate to the church in exchange for the church issuing a charitable gift annuity for the donor, agreeing to pay the donor a fixed income for a lifetime, regardless of fluctuating market conditions, payable monthly, quarterly, or annually. By prudently investing the proceeds from the church's sale of the donor's real estate, an income stream is generated to apply toward those payments.

> But a male age 80 would receive
> 8% annually, in recognition that
> his life expectancy is less.

If issued at a later age, the annual income to the donor would generally be far greater than what he could expect in interest from a bank. In early 2005 the charitable gift annuity rate for a male age 50 would be 5.3%, based on the rates established by the American Council on Gift Annuities that many major charities use. But a male, age 80, would receive 8% annually, in recognition that his life expectancy is less. For the right donor, this can be an important boost in monthly income, at a time of life when it is really needed.

By contributing the real estate to the church in exchange

for the annuity, the donor pays no capital gains tax at the time of transfer the church. If the donor has owned the real estate for more than one year, he also receives a major tax benefit in the year of the sale by receiving a donation credit for the gift portion of the appreciated fair market value of the property over his cost. Moreover, a part of his annual income is taxed at the lower capital gains rate, as capital gain payout, and part is tax-free for the term of his life expectancy. Thereafter, the income would be taxable as ordinary income. The amount of the first year donation credit is calculated as the present value of the church's remainder interest, based on IRS tables of life expectancy. Powerful software is available from Crescendointer active.com to calculate the benefits and explain this in detail to the church's and donor's tax advisors.

> ... it is mandatory that the church
> have expert legal and tax counsel in
> setting up any annuity program.

Donors like charitable gift annuities because they enable them to increase their income, decrease taxes and bless ministry. Upon the donor-annuitant's death, the church stops the payments, and any residual value belongs to the church. If your church wants to reduce the risk of making the payments, then you might consider reinsuring the risk by purchasing a commercial annuity from a life insurance company, In this case you are paid by the life insurance company each month an amount equal to the payment you must pay to the annuitant. You may not merely have the life insurance pay the payment directly, as the church cannot absolve its responsibility for the payment. If the life insurance company fails, unlikely as that may be, the church remains responsible for the payment to the annuitant. A commercial annuity or any specific asset may not be pledged to secure the donee organization's obligation to the annuitant. All of the organization's assets are backing for its unsecured obligation to the annuitant.

> Upon the donor-annuitant's death, the church stops the annuity payments, and any residual value belongs to the church.

Typically, a church could expect to have 15% to 25% of the proceeds of the real estate sale left over after fully funding the reinsurance premium for the amounts due its annuitant. Experts say that weighing all the financial factors—average mortality, the investment income, and the lifetime payout—it is like receiving a gift equal to about 50% of the original value of the real estate, if the church does not elect to pay to reinsure the risk. If a church does not reinsure, but issues a charitable gift annuity in the amount of $200,000, it may invest the real estate sale proceeds prudently, pay the donor payments for a lifetime, and, on the average, realize a gift that has a net value of about $100,000. Thus, by assuming the risk of the donor's long life, the church can, on the average, over many lives, net more than by reinsuring.

Issuing annuities to a large number of annuitants, your comfort level should rise as the church's experience approaches the averages experienced by insurance companies. Always reinsure the larger annuities to reduce exposure to risk. Your own experience should resemble the insurance company's mortality tables, as the law of large numbers begins to work in your favor.

> Issuing annuities to a large number of annuitants, your comfort level should rise as the church's experience approaches the averages experienced by insurance companies. Always reinsure the larger annuities to reduce exposure to risk.

There are several states that, by statute, do not regulate churches in the issuance of annuities. For example the State Regulations Committee of the American Council on Gift Annuities reported on its website at www.acga-web.org that as of April 15, 2005, Ohio law did not specifically address charitable gift annuities, but they add that the user of that information is solely responsible for determining and verifying it. Even if your state does not regulate church-issued annuities, proper reserves must be established and maintained, for the protection of the annuitant.

In certain states real estate may not be used to fund charitable gift annuities.

Bruce E. Bigelow, a founding partner of Charitable Development Consulting said, "For New York residents, and for many others, installment bargain sales may provide a much more reasonable alternative to the charitable gift annuity as a way of structuring a life income gift, while still protecting the interests of the charity."

> Even if your state does not regulate church-issued annuities, proper reserves must be established and maintained, for the protection of the annuitant.

Charitable gifts of real estate have increased dramatically over the years. Between 1998 and 2002, the Columbus Foundation received 12 donations totaling $2.5 million. In 2003 alone they received nine gifts of real estate gifts, for a total of $20.3 million. (*Columbus Dispatch* 02/19/2004.)

The author emphasizes that it is mandatory that the church have expert legal and tax counsel in setting up any annuity program.

Consider the following hypothetical case of John and Mary Jones, as illustrated by Crescendo software, showing the benefits to a husband wife, both age 75, donating real estate valued at $1,000,000, with an adjusted basis of $300,000. They would receive $63,000 every year, as long as either of them is living.

Wealth Replacement

With any major gift to charity, the losers could be the heirs. But the heirs may not lose, if the donor purchases a wealth replacement life insurance policy. The donor can use part of the cash tax savings to pay toward the premium on such a policy for the benefit of his heirs. Everyone wins.

<u>Charitable Gift Annuity</u>

Prepared for

John Jones
and
Mary Jones

A SERVICE PROVIDED BY

Crescendo Software
Planned Giving
110 Camino Ruiz
Camarillo California
Phone 800-858-9154
Crescendo@Cresmail.com

This illustration is offered as a service.
Please feel free to call for further assistance.

Software by Crescendo Inc.   Version 2005.1 Copyright © 2005

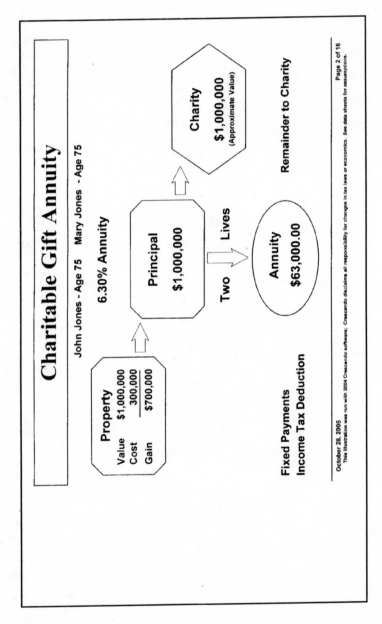

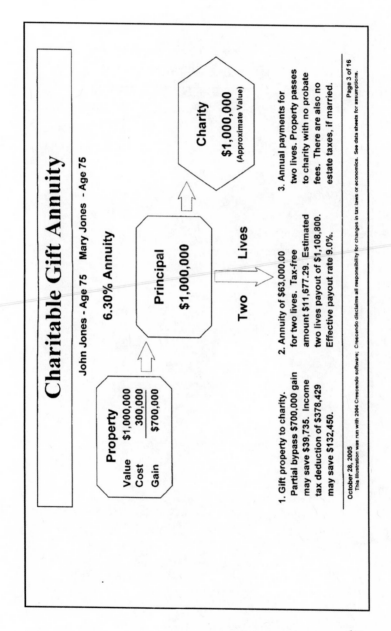

Charitable Gift Annuity

John Jones - Age 75   Mary Jones - Age 75

6.30% Annuity

Property

Value $1,000,000
Cost   300,000
Gain $700,000

Principal
$1,000,000

Two   Lives

Charity
$1,000,000
(Approximate Value)

1. Gift property to charity. Partial bypass $700,000 gain may save $39,735. Income tax deduction of $378,429 may save $132,450.

2. Annuity of $63,000.00 for two lives. Tax-free amount $11,677.29. Estimated two lives payout of $1,108,800. Effective payout rate 9.0%.

3. Annual payments for two lives. Property passes to charity with no probate fees. There are also no estate taxes, if married.

October 28, 2005   Page 3 of 16
This illustration was run with 2004 Crescendo software; Crescendo disclaims all responsibility for changes in tax laws or economics. See data sheets for assumptions.

CHARITABLE GIFT ANNUITY

FIRST PERSON	John Jones	AGE __75__
SECOND PERSON	Mary Jones	AGE __75__

GIFT AMOUNT	$1,000,000.00
CHARITABLE DEDUCTION	$378,429.40
ANNUITY OF 6.300%	$63,000.00
EXCLUSION RATIO	61.70%
EFFECTIVE ANNUITY RATE	9.0%

INCOME TAX INFORMATION

	ANNUAL PAYMENT	ANNUAL TOTALS
Ordinary Income	$24,129.00	$24,129.00
Capital Gain Payout	$27,193.71	$27,193.71
Tax Free*	$11,677.29	$11,677.29
ANNUITY AMOUNT	$63,000.00	$63,000.00

* Tax Free Until 2022

This illustration was run with 2004 Crescendo software; Crescendo disclaims all responsibility for changes in tax laws or economics.

CHARITABLE GIFT ANNUITY

The Charitable Gift Annuity is a combination of a gift to charity and an annuity. For senior persons, annuity rates may be 8%, 9% or even higher. Since part of the annuity payment is tax-free return of principal, the gift annuity may provide the annuitants with a substantial income. The combination of partially tax free income and the initial charitable deduction makes this agreement quite attractive. And after all payments have been made for the lives of the two annuitants, a favorite charity will benefit from the charitable gift.

Partly Tax Free Payments

A gift annuity is a contract between the charity and the individual. The individual, referred to as the donor, transfers property to the charity and the charity promises to pay a given amount at the end of each selected payment period to one annuitant for life or two annuitants for both lives. Part of the payment is interest earned and is taxable as ordinary income. Part of each payment is return of principal and is tax free. However, if an annuitant survives past his or her life expectancy, all later annuity payments will be ordinary income.

Gifted Property

Cash or appreciated property may be transferred to charity in exchange for a gift annuity. With appreciated property, a portion of the capital gains tax is avoided. Part of the gain is allocated to the charitable gift amount and there is no capital gains tax on that portion. The rest of the gain is allocated to the annuity portion and is taxed each year over the projected life expectancy of the annuitant. Since the tax is spread out over the life of the annuitant, and the annuitant is receiving in part tax free income, the transfer of appreciated property in exchange for a gift annuity can generate very favorable results.

Fixed Payments

Gift annuities are most attractive to senior persons. The annuity amount is fixed and will not change regardless of current investment or market conditions. Since the more senior person is probably more easily able to plan for the future with a fixed payment, the gift annuity seems most appropriate for a senior individual.

CHARITABLE GIFT ANNUITY

Two Lives

Donor	**John Jones**	Gift Amount	**$1,000,000.00**	Gift Date **05/12/2005**
First Person	**John Jones**	Birth Date	**01/01/1930**	
Second Person	**Mary Jones**	Birth Date	**01/01/1930**	Date of **05/12/2006**
Cost Basis	**$300,000.00**			First Ann. Payment
Payment Freq.	**ANNUAL**	(Payments at End of Selected Period)		

Annuity%		**6.300** %	
(A) Annual Annuity Payout		$63,000.00	(A)
Gift Amt. x Annuity %			
(B) Factor Age1 75			
Age2 75		9.8662	(B)
(IRS Pub. 1457, Table R(2), ((1-Factor)/AFR)			
AFR of the Month 5.0%			
(C) Adjustment for time of Payment		1.0000	(C)
(IRS Pub 1457, Table K)			

	End of Period	
1	1.0000	Annual
2	1.0123	Semi-Annual
3	1.0186	Quarterly
4	1.0227	Monthly

(D) Adjusted Factor		9.8662	(D)
Line (B) x Line (C)			
(E) Present Value of Annuity		$621,570.60	(E)
Line (D) x Line (A)			
(F) Amount Transferred		$1,000,000.00	(F)
(G) CHARITABLE GIFT VALUE		$378,429.40	(G)
Line (F) less Line (E)			

User Selected Annuity Rate

This illustration was run with 2004 Crescendo software; Crescendo disclaims all responsibility for changes in tax laws or economics.

CHARITABLE GIFT ANNUITY

Two Lives

(H) Unadjusted Expected Return Multiple	16.5	(H)
(Reg.Sec. 1.72-9, Table VI)		
(I) Adjustment if Not Monthly	-0.5	(I)
(Reg.Sec. 1.72-5(a)(2))		
(J) Adjusted Expected Return Multiple	16.0	(J)
Line (H) Plus Line (I)		
Sec. 72 Exp.16.0 -- Uniform Table Expectancy 17.6		
(K) Expected Return	$1,008,000.00	(K)
Line (J) Times Line (A)		
(L) EXCLUSION RATIO	61.7%	(L)
Line (E) Divided By Line (K)		
(M) Amt Excluded From Ordinary Taxation	$38,871.00	(M)
Exclusion Ratio Times Annuity		
Line (L) Times Line (A)		
(I.R.C. Sec. 72(b)(3))		
(N) Basis Allocated to Annuity	$186,471.18	(N)
Basis Times Line (E)/GIFT		
(O) Gain Allocated to Annuity	$435,099.42	(O)
Line (E) Less Line (N)		
(P) Gain Each Year	$27,193.71	(P)
Line (O) Divided By Line (J)		
(Not to Exceed Line (M); Assumption: Joint Property)		
(Reg.Sec. 1.1011-2(a)(4))		

SUMMARY OF ANNUITY

CHARITABLE DEDUCTION		$378,429.40	
EXCLUSION RATIO UNTIL 2022		61.7%	

INCOME TAX	PRO RATA FIRST PAYMENT	EACH PAYMENT	ANNUAL
Ord.Income	$0.00	24129.0000	$24,129.00
Cap. Gain	$0.00	27193.7100	$27,193.71
Tax Free	$0.00	11677.2900	$11,677.29
Ann. Amt	$0.00	63,000.00	$63,000.00

CHARITABLE GIFT ANNUITY

First Person	**John Jones**	Birth Date	**1/1/1930** Gift Date **5/12/2005**
Second Person	**Mary Jones**	Birth Date	**1/1/1930** Date of **5/12/2006**
Cost Basis	**$300,000.00**	Gift Amount	**$1,000,000.00** First Ann. Payment
Payment Freq.	**ANNUAL**	(Payments at End of Selected Period)	

Effective Equivalent Annuity Rate Calculation

(A) Annual Annuity	$63,000.00	(A)
(B) Exclusion Ratio	61.7%	(B)
(C) Excluded Amount	$38,871.00	(C)
Line (A) x Line (B)		
(D) Capital Gain Each Year	$27,193.71	(D)
Tax Rate 15.00%		
(E) Equivalent Amount of Ordinary Income	$35,561.01	(E)
(F) Return of Principal Each Year	$11,677.29	(F)
(G) Equivalent Amount of Ordinary Income	$17,965.06	(G)
(Line F /(1-35.00% Tax Rate))		
(H) Total Equivalent of Ordinary Income	$77,655.07	(H)
(I) Effective Amount Transferred	$867,550.00	(I)
(Gift Amount Less Tax Savings)		
(J) Effective Equivalent Annuity Rate		
(Line H/Line I)	8.95%	(J)
(Compared to Taxable Investments)	$89,510.77	
(K) Effective Equivalent Annuity Rate		
(Line H * (1-Tax rate)/Line I)	5.82%	(K)
(Compared to Tax Free Investments)	$58,182.00	

Summary	Tax Savings	Effective Rate
Initial Rate		6.30%
Income Tax Saving	$132,450	7.26%
Capital Gain Payout	$8,367	8.23%
Tax Free Payout	$6,288	8.95%

This illustration was run with 2004 Crescendo software; Crescendo disclaims all responsibility for changes in tax laws or economics.

CHARITABLE GIFT ANNUITY - INCOME TAXATION

Prepared For John and Mary Jones

			Annuity	$63,000.00
			Char. Gift	$378,429.40
			Capital Gain	$435,099.42
	TOTAL AMOUNT	$1,000,000.00	Basis	$186,471.18

Years	ORDINARY INCOME	CAPITAL GAIN PAYOUT	TAX FREE RETURN	CUMULATIVE CAPITAL GAIN	CUMULATIVE TAX FREE
2006	$24,129.00	$27,193.71	$11,677.29	$27,193.71	$11,677.29
2007	24,129.00	27,193.71	11,677.29	54,387.42	23,354.58
2008	24,129.00	27,193.71	11,677.29	81,581.13	35,031.87
2009	24,129.00	27,193.71	11,677.29	108,774.84	46,709.16
2010	24,129.00	27,193.71	11,677.29	135,968.55	58,386.45
2011	24,129.00	27,193.71	11,677.29	163,162.26	70,063.74
2012	24,129.00	27,193.71	11,677.29	190,355.97	81,741.03
2013	24,129.00	27,193.71	11,677.29	217,549.68	93,418.32
2014	24,129.00	27,193.71	11,677.29	244,743.39	105,095.61
2015	24,129.00	27,193.71	11,677.29	271,937.10	116,772.90
2016	24,129.00	27,193.71	11,677.29	299,130.81	128,450.19
2017	24,129.00	27,193.71	11,677.29	326,324.52	140,127.48
2018	24,129.00	27,193.71	11,677.29	353,518.23	151,804.77
2019	24,129.00	27,193.71	11,677.29	380,711.94	163,482.06
2020	24,129.00	27,193.71	11,677.29	407,905.65	175,159.35
2021	24,494.46	27,193.71	11,311.83	435,099.36	186,471.18
2022	62,999.94	0.06	0.00	435,099.42	186,471.18
2023	63,000.00	0.00	0.00	435,099.42	186,471.18
2024	63,000.00	0.00	0.00	435,099.42	186,471.18
2025	63,000.00	0.00	0.00	435,099.42	186,471.18
2026	63,000.00	0.00	0.00	435,099.42	186,471.18
2027	63,000.00	0.00	0.00	435,099.42	186,471.18
2028	63,000.00	0.00	0.00	435,099.42	186,471.18
2029	63,000.00	0.00	0.00	435,099.42	186,471.18
2030	63,000.00	0.00	0.00	435,099.42	186,471.18
2031	63,000.00	0.00	0.00	435,099.42	186,471.18
2032	63,000.00	0.00	0.00	435,099.42	186,471.18
2033	63,000.00	0.00	0.00	435,099.42	186,471.18
2034	63,000.00	0.00	0.00	435,099.42	186,471.18
2035	63,000.00	0.00	0.00	435,099.42	186,471.18
2036	63,000.00	0.00	0.00	435,099.42	186,471.18
2037	63,000.00	0.00	0.00	435,099.42	186,471.18
2038	63,000.00	0.00	0.00	435,099.42	186,471.18
2039	63,000.00	0.00	0.00	435,099.42	186,471.18
2040	63,000.00	0.00	0.00	435,099.42	186,471.18
2041	63,000.00	0.00	0.00	435,099.42	186,471.18
2042	63,000.00	0.00	0.00	435,099.42	186,471.18
2043	63,000.00	0.00	0.00	435,099.42	186,471.18
2044	63,000.00	0.00	0.00	435,099.42	186,471.18
2045	63,000.00	0.00	0.00	435,099.42	186,471.18

Note: Tax-Free return of basis not recovered by date of death may be deducted on last income tax return. See IRC Sec. 72(b).

– Oct 28, 2005
This illustration was run with 2004 Crescendo software; Crescendo disclaims all responsibility for changes in tax laws or economics.

CHARITABLE GIFT ANNUITY

Explanation for the Professional Advisor of John and Mary Jones

A. Flow Charts

The first flow chart for the gift annuity includes three boxes. The first indicates the initial circumstance for the property valued at $1,000,000. After transfer from the donors to the charity for the gift annuity contract, the charity is obligated to make payments of the annuity amounts for two lives. When all income payments have been completed, the balance of the value is available to the charity for its charitable purposes. As time passes, the boxes move progressively lower to show a change of ownership with the passage of time.

Under the first box in the second flow chart, the $1,000,000 is transferred to charity in the gift annuity contract. A gift annuity is a contract that obligates the charity to make the payments. While charities may be required by state insurance commissioners to maintain a reserve fund, the contractual obligation is against not only any reserve fund, but also the entire assets of the charitable organization. This feature makes gift annuities a very safe agreement for parties dealing with responsible charities, since most charitable entities have substantial assets.

When a gift annuity is created, the value of the annuity contract is determined under Section 72 of the Internal Revenue Code and the tables thereunder, and the other portion of the value is treated as a current charitable gift. There is a partial bypass of gain if appreciated property is transferred in exchange for a gift annuity. The appreciation allocable proportionately to the gift amount is bypassed.

In this illustration, there is a partial bypass of the gain and this saves $39,735 that would otherwise be payable in capital gains taxes. In addition, the gift value of this deduction is $378,429 and, at a marginal tax rate of 35.00%, the income tax savings are $132,450. Since this is an appreciated type deduction, this amount may be used up to 30% of adjusted gross income in the year of the gift. Any amount in excess of the 30% of A.G.I. limitation may be carried forward for as many as five years.

The center section of the chart shows the annuity payout percentage of 6.30%. Multiplying this number by the value of the property produces an annuity of $63,000.00 payable annual payments to the annuitants for two lives.

Because a portion of the value of the property is allocated to the annuity and this portion is returned under the Section 72 rules to the annuitants over two lifetimes, part of the annuity payment represents nontaxable return of principal. The tax free amount in this case is $11,677.29 per year. Over the two lives the basis allocated to the annuity will be recovered tax free.

Using the Treasury Uniform Table for these annuitants, this contract will last 17.6 years, and should pay out approximately $1,108,800. This payout, considering the income

• 74

tax savings from the deduction and the partly tax free payments, is comparable to receiving a taxable payout of 9.0%.

The third box shows the eventual distribution to the charity of approximately $1,000,000. This property will be transferred with no probate cost and, if the two parties are married, no estate taxes.

B. Gift Annuity Summary Sheet

The summary sheet is intended to be a simple outline of the major tax benefits for this agreement. It lists the names, the ages, the gift amount and the charitable income tax deduction. The annuity of 6.30% is based upon ages and total projected return, and an exclusion ratio of 61.7% is calculated. Once again, considering income tax savings and the partially tax free payments, the effective rate compared to a taxable investment is equivalent to a return of 9.0%.

The lower portion of this form details the income tax information for each payment and for the full year. An annual annuity payment is divided into the portion which represents the ordinary income earned on the investment in the contract, any capital gain amount prorated over two lives, and the tax free return of basis.

The asterisk adjacent to the tax free entry notes that the tax free amount continues only until the projected expectancy of the annuitants in the year 2022. If they live past this year, then all basis will have been recovered and the balance of all payments will be ordinary income.

C. Deduction Calculation

The deduction calculation for the gift annuity proceeds through three different phases. The first section determines the value of the annuity and the charitable gift amount. The second section determines the expectancy and total payment to calculate the exclusion ratio. A third section calculates the anticipated capital gain for any exchange of an appreciated asset for a gift annuity. Finally, there is a summary of the annuity.

In the upper section are listed the names, birth dates, gift date and date of first annuity payment. The date of first annuity payment must be within the first period under the payment frequency. Since this annuity pays annually, the date of first payment must be within twelve months of the funding date.

The remaining sections of the calculation follow lines "A" through lines "P".

A. Annual Payout: The gift annuity value times the annuity percentage produces the annual payout. This amount is rounded up to the nearest two, four or twelve cents, in order to insure that all period payments, whether semiannually, quarterly or monthly, will be of exactly the same amount to the exact cent, thus simplifying administration.

B. Deduction Factor The deduction factor from table S is subtracted from one
IRS Pub. 1457 and then divided by the AFR.

75 •

C. Adjustment for Time of Payment:
If the annuity is paid semiannually, quarterly or monthly, the annuitant has received the value of interest earnings during the year and this is the adjustment for that interest.

D. Adjusted Factor:
Initial factor times the adjustment for the period of payment.

E. Present Value of Annuity:
The actuarial value under Treasury tables for an annuity contract payment, paying the annuity on Line (A).

F. Amount Transferred:
Value of property exchanged for annuity.

G. Charitable Gift Value:
Subtracting the contract value from the property value results in the gift value. This is the IRS's assumed value of the contribution to charity, measured in present value terms.

H. Unadjusted Return Multiple:
The approximate number of years that the annuitants are expected to live.

I. Adjustments If Not Monthly:
A correction for quarterly, semiannual or annual payments.

J. Adjusted Expected Return Multiple:
The unadjusted multiple adjusted for the selected period. The next line shows both the Sec. 72 Return Multiple and the Treasury Uniform Table expectancy of 17.6 years.

K. Expected Return:
Multiplying the multiple of Line (J) times the annuity payout produces an estimate of the total anticipated payment to the donors.

L. Exclusion Ratio:
The Line (E) value of the contract divided by the Line (K) total payout enables allocation of return of principal on an annual basis. This allocation is expressed as a percentage and multiplied by the annual payout to determine the return of principal portion. The return of principal portion is then further divided into the part that is capital gain prorated over two lives and the part that is tax free return of basis.

M. Amount Excluded, Ordinary Taxation:
The Line (M) value is Line (L) times the annual annuity and represents the return of principal each year.

N. Basis Allocated to Annuity:
The basis is prorated proportionately between the Line (E) contract value and the Line (G) gift value.

O. Gain Allocated:
The Line (E) contract value less the prorated basis is the gain to be recognized pro rata over two lives.

P. Gain Each Year:
Dividing the total gain by the adjusted multiple of Line (J) illustrates the amount to be recognized each year. With a two-life annuity and separate property, the divisor will be the one-life multiple rather than the two-life.

The Summary of Annuity section repeats the above information in a more organized format. The charitable deduction is $378,429. Since the exclusion ratio until year 2022 is 61.7%, the lower portion of this spreadsheet allocates the payments accordingly.

The annual payment is allocated 61.7% to the total amount of gain and tax free return. Based upon any gain recognized on Line (P), the balance of the 61.7% is tax free. All remaining payment is ordinary income. Amounts in this contract are thus $24,129.00 of ordinary income, $27,193.71 of prorated gain and $11,677.29 of tax free return.

Since the exact amounts to the precise cent are reported by the charity to the donors and a recipient may not receive exactly a full year's payments the initial year of the agreement, there is also a division into prorata first payment and a payment for each period, in this case the annually amounts.

If the donors create an agreement less than one full period from the desired payout date, then there can be a prorated first payment for the short period. In addition, if the agreement is not funded in January of a given year, there may be fewer than the normal number of payments in the first year for all except annuities with annual payments. The breakout between ordinary income, capital gain and tax free return is thus calculated taking into account potential partial payments.

D. Equivalent Annuity Rate

The equivalent rate form details the calculation necessary to determine equivalent return rate in order to compare a gift annuity with other types of taxable payouts. This calculation starts with the annuity amount and determines the excluded amount on Line (C). Line (D) lists any prorated gain amount reported each year. Since gain can potentially be subject to a different tax rate (in this case 15.00% as opposed to 35.00% on ordinary income) the capital gain amount in Line (D) represents an equivalent value of $35,561.01 if it were ordinary income.

The return of principal on Line (F) is the equivalent of a tax free payment and equates to $17,965.06 on Line (G). Adding Line (G) and Line (E) to the annual ordinary income, the total equivalent ordinary income is $77,655.07.

Since the contribution of $1,000,000 results in an income tax deduction of $378,429 and the anticipated tax savings are therefore $132,450, the actual net investment is reduced from $1,000,000 by the tax savings to $867,550.00. Dividing $77,655.07 on Line (H) by $867,550.00 on Line (I) produces an effective equivalent annuity rate of 8.95%. In addition, multiplying the Line (H) value by 1 less the tax rate and then dividing it by Line (I) results in the equivalent tax free rate of 5.82%. These rates are usually quite helpful in illustrating the benefits of the gift annuity agreement.

E. Income Taxation

The final spreadsheet is a detailed form that lists the exact amount of ordinary income, capital gain and tax free return to be reported to the IRS each year that the annuity is in existence. At the top center are listed the annuity payment, the gift value and the capital gain and cost basis allocated to the annuity. This capital gain and cost basis will be prorated and recovered during the lives of the two donors.

In 2006, there is recovery of ordinary income of $24,129.00, prorated gain of $27,193.71 and tax free return of $11,677.29. The fifth column shows the cumulative capital gain recovery and the sixth column shows the cumulative tax free. In the second and later years of the agreement, the full annual amounts are displayed for the ordinary income, gain and tax free return. Once again, columns 5 and 6 display the cumulative recovery of prorated gain and cumulative recovery of tax free payments. By the year 2022, the prorated gain and tax free amounts at the top of the spreadsheet are nearing completion of recovery and there may be a partial recovery of the final amounts of prorated gain and tax free payments in that year. After all gain and tax free portions have been recovered, then any future payments are fully ordinary income.

Three additional gift annuity rules should be noted. First, if both gift annuitants die prior to the full recovery of the tax free portion, then under I.R.C. Section 72(b) the unrecovered amount is a permissible tax deduction on the final year tax return. Second, if appreciated property is given by a donor-annuitant, recognized annual gain is limited to annual return of principal. Third, a married couple may prorate their gain amounts evenly over the two life expectancy. However, if separate property is used to fund a two life agreement, the prorated gain is recognized during the first life and the return of principal amount may be totally capital gain until all gain has been recognized. Following the recovery in subsequent years of all return of principal, the annuity payments eventually become fully ordinary income as before.

F. Program Options

Several options are available with the gift annuity. One can select reinsurance if the annuity contract specifies that the annuity must be reinsured. This reinsurance plan then enables one to use the exact amount paid for reinsurance to value the annuity, with the remaining value equaling the charitable gift.

The options also enable one to select either separate or joint property for a two life gift annuity. Ordinarily, with a husband and wife, joint property is the usual selection. However, with a parent and child, separate property is generally appropriate. Finally, if the standard payment period is within 2 or 3 days of the actual time prior to the selected payout date, the program does not automatically select a prorata payment. However, there is an option that can be used to mandate a prorata payment if desired in a particular illustration.

There is also an option to calculate the end of contract value to charity. Most charitable organizations leave the end of contract value in the default position and show an approximate value to the charity equal to the initial contribution. This is a marketing solution that simplifies the illustration. However, it is possible to calculate, based on the estimated return rate of the annuity reserve fund and the actual payout over the projected two lives, the exact projected benefit to the charity. This calculated amount will accurately reflect projected increases or decreases in the principal amount distributed to charity at the end of the agreement.

CHARITABLE GIFT ANNUITY

Rate of the		First	
Month **5**		Paydate	**5/12/2006**
Donor **John Jones**		Income Tax %	**35.00** %
First **John Jones**		Cap. Gain %	**15.00** %
Person		(Income and capital gains rates are assumed.)	
Birth **1/1/1930**		Property Amount	**$1,000,000**
Date			
2nd **Mary Jones**		Cost Basis	**$300,000**
Person			
Birth **1/1/1930**		Current Return	**0.00** %
Date			
Freq. **ANNUAL**		Annuity %	**6.30** %
Gift **5/12/2005**		Amt to Charity	**$1,000,000**
Date			
	Options: **Two Life Annuity**		

GIFT ANNUITY - Deduction vs. Tax Free Income

	0.05	0.05	0.05
Char. Deduction	$378,429.40	$378,429.40	$378,429.40
Exclusion Ratio %	61.7%	61.7%	61.7%
Capital Gain Pmts	$27,193.71	$27,193.71	$27,193.71
Tax Free Income	$11,677.29	$11,677.29	$11,677.29

This illustration was run with 2004 Crescendo software; Crescendo disclaims all responsibility for changes in tax laws or economics.

• 80

PART THREE

Operations

~

"Ye have not because ye ask not."

- James 4:2 (KJV))

Chapter 9

How to Ask
for the Gift

*"You make a living by what you get . . . but
you make a life by what you give."*
- Sir Winston Churchill, statesman, historian,
and biographer. (1874-1965)

GEORGE BARNA SAID: "MOST PASTORS, CHURCH STAFF AND
lay leaders are both inadequately trained and emotionally
unprepared for communicating about and actually raising the
kind of money required to lead a church toward the fulfillment of its vision." George Barna, *How to Increase Giving in
Your Church* (Ventura, California: Regal Books, 1997), 13

"Most pastors, church staff and lay
leaders are both inadequately
trained and emotionally unprepared
for communicating about and
actually raising the kind of money
required to lead a church toward
the fulfillment of its vision."

~ George Barna

The big real estate sign in front of the property can be
your first indication that the seller-donor might be a candidate
to make a partial gift at this time. Timing is everything, and
when the property is listed for sale is the prime moment for
the seller-donor to consider your request. Read that sentence
again at least twice. When you see the "For Sale" sign in front
of the property that meets your requirements, just think to
yourself, "that sign should say instead in big bold letters:
"PHILANTHROPY IN PROGRESS, CALL 555-5555."

After all, the big sign in front of
the property is how you got the big
idea that the seller-donor might
well be a candidate to make the
partial gift at this time.

The listing Realtor will be one of the seller's advisors,
required by law to represent the seller's best interests. If you are
trying this on your own, it would be well to meet with him

early in the process to explain some of the intricacies and extra benefits, because this will likely be the Realtor's first exposure to philanthropy involving real estate.

> ... just think to yourself, that sign should say instead in big bold letters: "PHILANTHROPY FOR THE ASKING, CALL 555-5555"

According to George Brakely, in *Tested Ways to Successful Fund Raising*, New York: AMACOM, A division of American Management Associations, New York, 1980, page 26, the following were included in "factors in motivating donors to support the institution:

1. Individuals, corporations, and foundations have money to give.

2. The right person or persons ask them, at the right time, and in the right circumstances.

3. People have a sincere desire to help other people.

4. People wish to belong to or be identified with a group or organization they admire."

The real estate proposal should be prepared by your own legal counsel, stipulating that the transaction shall be structured to qualify as a Bargain Sale transaction pursuant to the Internal Revenue Code. Your lawyer should coordinate with the seller's lawyer to specify in the purchase contract that the seller declares his donative intent. This would be a good time for you to consider engaging a Realtor knowledgeable in these real estate matters to represent the church's interests alone in regard to the real estate.

Homework Assignment

"No cow will let down her milk in response to a letter
or a phone call. You have got to sit down beside her
and go to work."

- James R. Reynolds, leading
Harvard University's successful $82 million
fund-raising campaign.

Place sufficient emphasis on ministries to the broader community reaching people who are poor, sick, or in prison. That will appeal to those donors who are not sitting in your pew on Sunday.

Have a vision casting meeting to develop the core principles which will guide the organization in all its decisions. Always bearing in mind the standard set by those abiding principles, the methods and strategies can be developed to facilitate the missions your church would carry out, if funds were available. Bring together to your key leaders: the board members, teachers, administrators, and various committee members, a core group of perhaps 12 to 20 members. Determine who you are as a church, and whom you are trying to serve. Prioritize goals according to their importance. Explain that your ultimate goal will be to rank their projects in order of necessity and desirability in broad categories. This may mean that several buildings may need to acquired or constructed in several phases. After prioritizing them, then determine the space requirements for the most important one. Then have a free-ranging brainstorm session to list all the possible uses for the most important new facility and from that discussion, create a wish list. Without pausing to assess or reject the merits of each item, just write each item on a chalkboard until you have 25 or 30 ideas, some good, and some not so good. Make sure everybody gets an opportunity to contribute potential uses. From this list of uses, possibly with the help of an architect or someone knowledgeable in space requirements and costs, estimate the size and cost of your dream project. As is often the case, the cost of the dream list is too high and therefore the list must be prioritized into A, B, and C categories, where A is absolutely necessary; B is highly desirable, and C would be the "frosting on the cake": nice but not essential. Perhaps more space for seating in the auditorium would be absolutely essential, and be shown on the A list. Should the auditorium or fellowship hall be a multipurpose room which could double as a gymnasium during the week, thereby facilitating community service and outreach? A larger nursery could be the key to attracting parents with small children. A larger narthex or lobby could be highly desirable so that congregants could meet to fellowship before and after worship service. Usually these interior space enhancements will necessitate more parking spaces. In today's highly mobile society it is often the case that while the zoning code may require one parking space for each three or four persons who can be seated in the auditorium; the church may require even more parking spaces because, for example, some families with three people arrive in three cars.

Have the design of your project illustrated and present them in a nice folio, complete with a well written narrative and photographs of people who would be leading in the various efforts. Place sufficient emphasis on ministries to the broader community reaching people who are poor, sick, or in prison. That will appeal to those donors who are not sitting in your pew on Sunday. For professional assistance in vision casting for your church or other nonprofit organization, contact Roger Walker at www.WalkerConsultingLLC.com.

"Rescue the Perishing"
- Fannie Crosby, writer of hymns.
(1820-1915)

In your folio preparation, start with your mission statement as to why the organization or the project was established. Explain the history of the organization and the qualifications of its leaders. Discuss the structure of the organization, outlining the involvement by board members, volunteers, and staff. Outline the goals that you intend to accomplish in line with your mission statement. State your objectives as to how many people you intend to help within what time frame. Finally, using the last annual financial statement as a frame of reference, explain how the contributions will be used, including budget projections.

Plans fail for lack of counsel,
but with many advisers they succeed.

-Solomon, in Proverbs 15:22 (NIV)

Chapter 10

NUTS AND BOLTS

AS SOON AS YOUR SELLER-DONOR SEES YOUR WRITTEN
Bargain Sale draft agreement, he is going to inevitably say, "I'll
check it out with my attorney and my CPA." Then the con-
sultation begins between his attorney and the church's
attorney. Happily, it very often meets everyone's goals. There
are intricacies that will pertain to each church and to the individual donor's particular circumstances. Any procedure
described in this book should only be done with the advice of
expert legal counsel. If you are generating a $250,000.00 gift,
don't begrudge the law firm's $5,000 fee for keeping you legal.
It's well worth every penny.

You might be thinking "Why doesn't the donor just give
us the property outright, all for free?" The truth is most

> # The truth is, most income-producing properties of this size and type have some debt already encumbering them, say, between 40% and 70%.

income-producing properties of this size and type have some debt already encumbering them, say, between 40% and 70%. This existing debt of the seller-donor typically has to be either assumed or paid off upon transfer. Even if a $4 million property is free and clear, it is very difficult to persuade your donor to give 100% to ministry. You might identify several potential bargain sale prospects while you are still looking for that one outright gift.

The Outright Gift Property Donor

The profile of the outright gift property donor might be a lifelong member of the church, with no heirs, who believes, rightly, that all we own is a gift from God. This person has long since embraced the truth promulgated in the beginning sentence of Rick Warren's all-time (in the history of the world!) best selling hardback book, *The Purpose Driven Life*. "It's not about you." Donors in this category will arrive at this pinnacle of major gifting after a series of steps in personal growth. They usually start with a faithful pattern of regular giving, followed perhaps a few years later with intermediate levels of occasional significant gifts, perhaps annually or on the occasion of a large charity project. Then they choose to give a once-in-a-lifetime gift of major proportions, such as the outright gift of a very valuable free-and-clear property. For more on this subject, read William T. Sturtevant's excellent work: *The Artful Journey: Cultivating and Soliciting the Major Gift.* Guided by a lifelong philosophy of giving inspired by the following passage from Proverbs 11:24 (NIV), the donor wishes, more than anything, upon his death, to bless ministry. "One man gives freely, yet gains even more; another withholds unduly, but comes to poverty."

Outsiders and Donative Intent

Would anyone outside our church membership make a property donation? Don't they have to be a member of my church or at least a member of our denomination? *Au Contraire!* The Salvation Army does not make you sit in a pew before they will accept a donation, and not just for a few bucks in the kettle, either. They accept huge real estate property donations.

> The Salvation Army does not make you sit in a pew before they will accept a donation, and not just for a few bucks in the kettle, either.

The IRS does require that the donor must have donative intent. The gift cannot be donated merely for financial or tax motivation. There have been court cases over just what is the definition of a gift. The meaning of the word "gift" has been analyzed in-depth, resulting in rulings that the motivation for a gift must include feelings of such imponderables as admiration, respect, appreciation, gratitude and the satisfaction that comes from making a difference in the lives of people. Even the most unrepentant sinner who has not darkened the doors of any church for years, except perhaps for a Christmas or Easter cantata, can respect the church and be grateful for the many contributions you make to the community. These every day good works are what scripture admonishes us to perform: provide food for the hungry and clothing for those in need. Visit those who are sick or in prison, and much more. Who can argue with that?

Jesus Christ said: "*Inasmuch as ye have done it unto one of the least of these my brethren, ye have done it unto me.*" Matthew 25:40 ((KJV)). You must give sufficient attention to developing the relationship of the real estate seller/donor with the church so as to establish the necessary element of donative intent for the bargain-sale to occur.

Even the most unrepentant sinner who has not darkened the doors of any church for years, except perhaps for a Christmas or Easter cantata, can respect the church . . .

The donor may consider the tax savings as one element to be weighed, as in the case of all good financial planning, but donative intent is mandatory. In fact, it must be demonstrated in some way before the consummation of the arrangement. The Lincoln Community Foundation advises that, "An important first step in planning bargain sales is to document in writing the donor's intent to make a charitable gift of the excess of the property's fair market value over the bargain sale price. A letter from the donor to the charity prior to the execution of the arrangement should document that intent." It should certainly be declared in the real estate purchase contract. On the other extreme, the IRS has successfully challenged certain donation deductions which were considered not to be based on charitable intent. For example, in Stubbs v. United States, a real estate developer dedicated a strip of his land to the state for a public roadway, for which he claimed a charitable contribution deduction. But the IRS argued successfully in tax court, affirmed by the Court of Appeals for the Ninth Circuit, that his intent was not purely donative, but that his true motivation included increasing the value of his remaining acreage, due to the new road to be constructed by the state, which would help him rezone his remaining acreage for a trailer park.

> . . . to be allowed based on the full appreciated value, the donor must have owned the real property for at least one year.

Section 170 of the Internal Revenue Code provides that in order for a donation deduction for a gift to a church to be allowed based on the full appreciated value, the donor must have owned the real property for at least one year. He may offset only 30% of Adjusted Gross Income in any one year, but may carry forward the unused deduction for up to 5 more years.

———————————

"You can tell more about the spiritual lives
of a couple by looking at their chequebook than
by anything else."

- Larry Burkett, Christian author and radio
personality. (1939-2003)

Chapter 11

TAXING MATTERS

THIS SECTION WILL INTRODUCE THE READER TO VARIOUS tax considerations affecting major real estate gifts to nonprofit organizations. For example, the Internal Revenue Service requires that certain forms be filed, both for the year in which real estate is donated to the charity and also upon any resale within two years. We will review the Federal taxation of income received by the charity which is not related to its tax exempt purposes, along with certain exemptions. Moreover, the utmost priority of protecting the tax exempt status of the nonprofit organization will be highlighted.

IRS Form 8283 must be filed when the deduction claimed for all non-cash charitable contributions totals more than $500, including real estate (see Form 8283 in appendix A).

Section B of Form 8283 is an appraisal summary for real estate in the amount of more than $5,000. It must be signed by three parties: the donor-taxpayer, the donee organization, and the appraiser. The donee organization must affirm that in the event it sells, exchanges, or otherwise disposes of the property within three years after the date of receipt, it will file Form 8282 Donee Information Return, with the IRS and give the donor a copy of that form (see appendix A). This acknowledgement does not represent agreement with the claimed fair market value. It does acknowledge receipt of the property. It also asks if the organization intends to use the property for an unrelated use. Obviously, if the property were later resold within three years for a price lower than the fair market appraised value originally claimed on Form 8283, the IRS would be very interested to learn that, and it might go back to the donor for an additional tax payment.

Unrelated Business Income Tax (UBIT)

A 501(C)(3) organization may become liable for Unrelated Business Income Tax ("UBIT") when it earns income from a trade or business that is unrelated to its tax-exempt purpose. However, if income-producing real estate is received as an outright gift free and clear of any indebtedness, the UBIT will not apply. If real estate is received in a bargain sale transaction, subject to the seller's mortgage more than 5 years old, and the seller has owned the property for more than 5 years, then generally, the rental income would not be subject to UBIT, so long as the property is resold within 10 years. However, if the nonprofit organization incurs "acquisition indebtedness", e.g., new financing, then UBIT would apply. IRC § 514(b). Such income is to be reported annually to the IRS on Form 990-T. The estimated taxes are payable quarterly.

Neighborhood Land Exception

There is a "Neighborhood Land" exception to such debt-financed property if the property is located near the tax-exempt organization and will be used within 10 years (15 years for churches). Citing IRC § 514 (b)(3), the website at the law firm of Hurwit & Associates, Legal counsel for philanthropy and nonprofit sector, says, *"The tax on unrelated debt-financed property does not apply to income from real property first, if the land is located in the neighborhood of other property used by the organization in furthering exempt purposes and, second, if the organization plans to use the property for exempt purposes within ten years."*

Protect the Exemption

If unrelated business income, (e.g., from apartments, office buildings or shopping centers) becomes a substantial portion of the exempt organization's total income received directly, the organization could conceivably lose its exemption. How much unrelated business income is substantial? There is no bright-line test as to the percentage of exempt income. Daniel D. Busby CPA, author of *The Zondervan Church and Nonprofit Organization Tax and Financial Guide 2001* edition, wrote, *"It is possible that the IRS will deny or revoke the tax-exempt status of an organization when it regularly derives over one-half of its annual revenue from unrelated activities."**

---

*From *The Zondervan Church and Nonprofit Organization Tax and Financial Guide 2001 edition*, Daniel D. Busby (Grand Rapids, Michigan: Zondervan Publishing House, a division of Harper Collins Publishers, 2001), p. 35. Used by permission of Zondervan Publishing House. All rights reserved.

Celia Roady, author of *UBIT Problems for Tax-Exempt Charitable Trusts for the Southern Federal Tax Institute*, 35th Annual Institute September 21, 2000, Atlanta, Georgia, said in regard to UBIT activities approaching 25% to 30% of overall revenues, *"it may be desirable to put them in a for-profit corporate subsidiary for liability protection reasons. . . . This is often a sensible approach from a business perspective, and it has the corollary benefit of protecting the organization from an IRS challenge to exemption."*

> "...it has the corollary benefit of protecting the organization from an IRS challenge to exemption."
> ~ Celia Roady

Establishing a For-Profit Subsidiary

Consider strongly having your legal counsel set up a separate for-profit subsidiary for each additional major real estate acquisition involving rental income, so as enhance the goal of isolating the liability exposure and to obtain the many other benefits it provides, even though its rental income may be taxable as UBIT. The Revenue Act of 1950 made taxable such a commercial and investment entity, known as a "feeder," established for the benefit of its tax exempt parent. Leading to passage of The Revenue Act of 1950 the Senate Report stated:

> *The problem at which the tax on unrelated business income is directed is primarily that of unfair competition. The tax-free status of [§501(c)(3)] organizations enables them to use their profits tax-free*

*to expand operations, while their competitors can
expand only with profits remaining after taxes. Also,
a number of examples have arisen where these organizations have, in effect, used their tax exemptions to
buy an ordinary business. That is, they have acquired
the business with little or no investment on their own
part and paid for it in installments out of subsequent
earnings–a procedure which could not be followed if
the business were taxable.*

*[T]his provision [does not] deny the exemption
where the organizations are carrying on unrelated
active business enterprises, nor require that they dispose of such businesses. It merely imposes the same tax
on income derived from an unrelated trade or business
as is born by their competitors. In fact it is not
intended that the tax imposed on unrelated business
income will have any effect on the tax-exempt status
of any organization. An organization which is exempt
prior to the enactment of this bill, if continuing the
same activities, would still be exempt after this bill
becomes law. In a similar manner any reasons for
denying exemption prior to the enactment of this bill
would continue to justify denial of exemption after the
bill's passage.*

S. Rep. No. 2375, 81st Cong., 2d Session. 28-9 (1950),
reprinted in 1950-2 C.B. 483, 504-05.

Hurwit & Associates, Legal counsel for philanthropy and
nonprofit sector, also wrote for its website at http://www.hur-
witassociates.com: *"Those relatively few organizations that do
lose their tax exemption each year are most often unable to show*

adherence to their basic charitable purposes. And in the majority of those cases, the IRS has revoked exemption due to intentional malfeasance or self-dealing. "

"If you are driving a car or a truck that weighs 9,800 pounds and you see a bridge that says limit 10,000 pounds, you go look for another bridge that says 20,000 pounds."

- Warren Buffett, explaining the concept of a margin of safety. 1997 speech at Caltech. Investor. (1930-

There are other factors in considering the exemption, such as time spent on charitable activities, ministry, etc. In a 1997 speech at Caltech, Warren Buffett paraphrased Benjamin Graham, saying "If you were driving a car or a truck that weighs 9,800 pounds and you see a bridge that says limit 10,000 pounds, you go look for another bridge that says 20,000 pounds." Be safe.

The income tax on the operation of the rental property would only be due on the net income at one entity level, not both. The subsidiary's net income after paying its taxes, would then be paid as a tax free dividend to the nonprofit organization. There is no double taxation in this arrangement.

Considering the deductibility for straight-line depreciation, a non-cash expense, and the payment for a building manager who is on the staff of a religious organization, there may not be much tax, if any, for several years, under a typical leveraged real estate investment. The position of the IRS on this point is demonstrated by the following example on page 18 of IRS Publication 598 (Rev. March 2005), in which it illustrates that the exempt organization's building manager is receiving $15,000 out of a total rental income of $20,000, thereby establishing a net loss of $2,500 after all other normal expenses:

> *"**Net operating loss.** If, after applying the debt/ basis percentage to the income from debt-financed property and the deductions directly connected with this income, the deductions exceed the income, an organization has a net operating loss for the tax year. This amount may be carried back or carried over to other tax years in the same manner as any other net operating loss of an organization with unrelated business taxable income. (For a discussion of the net operating loss deduction, see Modifications under Deductions earlier in this chapter.) However, the debt/basis percentage is not applied in those other tax years to determine the deductions that may be taken in those years.*
>
> ***Example.** Last year, Y, an exempt organization, **received $20,000 of rent from a debt-financed building that it owns.** (emphasis added). Y had no other unrelated business taxable income for the year. The deductions directly connected with this building were property taxes of $5,000, interest of $5,000 on the acquisition indebtedness, **and salary of $15,000 to the building manager.** (emphasis added). The debt/basis percentage with respect to the building was*

50%. Under these circumstances, Y must take into account, in computing its unrelated business taxable income, $10,000 (50% of $20,000) of income and $12,500 (50% of $25,000) of the deductions directly connected with that income.

Thus, Y sustained a net operating loss of $2,500 ($10,000 of income less $12,500 of deductions), which may be carried back or carried over to other tax years without further application of the debt/basis percentage."

Donor's Tax Write-Off

Consider the case of a hypothetical high income donor who sold his $1 million appreciated real property to a donee at a bargain sale price of $750,000. His cost basis was $400,000 after taking straight line depreciation. The capital gains rate is 15%. His cost basis will be adjusted in a bargain sale to a new basis by the same factor as the sale price bears to the FMV fair market value (750,000/1,000,000 = 75%).

So with a basis of $400,000, then his adjusted basis for this sale would be $300,000 and his taxable gain would be the amount received $750,000 minus the adjusted basis of $300,000, which is $450,000.

His 15% capital gains tax is $67,500. But his $250,000 donation deduction is calculated at ordinary rates, 35% of the $250,000, which produces a tax savings on his ordinary income equal to $87,500. He gets to keep the $750,000; plus he is has a net tax savings of $20,000. If he had sold the property for the full $1 million (a big if, considering all the imponderables of holding for resale), he would have paid a 15% capital gains tax on $600,000, which is $90,000, netting him $910,000. The difference is only $140,000, and it results in a very satisfying donation. Finally, many states also allow state income tax charitable deductions, that follow federal charitable deducibility guidelines, if itemized. Check with your C.P.A. first.

> He might easily have had to reduce his $1 million appraised value asking price by the end of the listing period, due to the vagaries of the marketplace, negotiating skill differentials, etc., and most importantly, ongoing opportunity cost.

He might easily have otherwise had to reduce his $1 million appraised value asking price by the end of the listing period, due to the vagaries of the marketplace, negotiating skill differentials, etc., and most importantly, ongoing opportunity cost. On the other hand, this bargain sale transaction and the cash to close it are available now, while the potential outright future sale is only conjecture. This rationale works very well, for donors with the right combination of donative intent and other circumstances.

Debt Encumbered Real Estate

When the donor donates real estate encumbered by debt, the loan balance is treated as an amount realized, and calculated by the donor just as if the donee had paid cash in the same amount as the indebtedness. Following is a discussion of the computation from an IRS Revenue Ruling: (Rev. Rul. 81-163; 1981-1 C.B. 433)

"FACTS

During the taxable year, an individual taxpayer transferred unimproved real property subject to an outstanding mortgage of 10x dollars to an organization described in section 170(c) of the Internal Revenue Code. On the date of transfer the fair market value of the property was 25x dollars, and the taxpayer's adjusted basis in the property was 15x dollars. The taxpayer had held the property for more than one year and made no other charitable contributions during the taxable year. The property was a capital asset in the taxpayer's hands. Thus, under the provisions of section 170 the taxpayer made a charitable contribution to the organization of 15x dollars (25x dollars fair market value less 10x dollars mortgage).

LAW AND ANALYSIS

Section 1011(b) of the Code and section 1.1011-2(b) of the Income Tax Regulations provide that, if a deduction is allowable under section 170 (relating to charitable contributions) by reason of a sale, the adjusted basis for determining the gain from the sale is the portion of the adjusted basis of the entire property that bears the same ratio to the adjusted basis as the amount realized bears to the fair market value of the entire property.

Section 1.1011-2(a)(3) of the regulations provides that, if property is transferred subject to an indebtedness, the amount of the indebtedness must be treated as an amount realized for purposes of determining whether there is a sale or exchange to which section 1011(b) of the Code and section 1.1011-2 apply, even though the transferee does not agree to assume or pay the indebtedness.

Because the outstanding mortgage of 10x dollars is treated as an amount realized, the taxpayer's adjusted basis for determining gain on the bargain sale is 6x dollars (15x dollars adjusted basis of the entire property X 10x dollars amount realized 25x dollars fair market value of the entire property).

HOLDING The taxpayer recognizes long-term capital gain of 4x dollars (10x dollars amount realized less 6x dollars adjusted basis) on the bargain sale of the property to the charitable organization."

Note: Revenue Rulings use a theoretical set of facts and apply the tax law; the ruling is fundamentally an illustration. If your particular set of facts are, to a large extent, the same as the set of facts in the ruling, you can be reasonably certain of the same outcome.

"Suppose one of you wants to build a tower.
Will he need not first sit down and estimate the
cost to see if he has enough money to complete it?"

- Luke 14:28 (NIV)

PART FOUR

Income-Producing
Gift Property

~

Chapter 12

VALUE: A PRIMER ON NET OPERATING INCOME

NOW, YOU MAY BE THINKING, "WHY DO WE WANT INCOME-producing property, even if it's free?" A huge stream of income will accompany some of your best and largest gift opportunities. You will use the stream of rental income from commercial tenants occupying from one half to three fourths of the space to pay the mortgage payment, while you make the remaining 25% to 50% of the space available for your new ministry. Or you may use the free space to bless other ministries and for outreach.

The free space is at no cost because the seller-donor contributed 25% to 50% of the property's value in his bargain-sale transaction for you. If you have no ministry ideas for the free space, then you can rent out the free space and use the cash flow to pay off any prior debt, or to fund staffing for increased ministry, or to bless other 501(C)(3) programs.

> If you have no ministry ideas for the free space, then you can rent out the free space and use the cash flow to pay off any prior debt.

Net Operating Income

Acquiring income property successfully requires understanding the financial fundamentals of property analysis. The basic measurement of profitability for income producing real estate is net operating income. The definition of net operating income is the projected income of the property after first deducting the stabilized operating expenses, vacancy and credit losses. It is different from the accounting concept of net profit in that operating expenses do not include either depreciation or interest expense. Net Operating Income is used to determine cash available before debt service.

Cash flow is the lifeblood of real estate investing, not necessarily a short term accounting of net profit. If a large part of your profit is being paid out monthly as the principal portion of a very large mortgage payment, then you may have an accounting profit but not necessarily any net cash flow.

Depreciation

Depreciation expense is a non-cash accounting item. You may deduct it for income tax purposes, but it does not neces-

Cash flow is the lifeblood of real estate investing, not necessarily a short-term accounting net profit.

sarily require a corresponding payment of cash. In a larger sense, it is true that the building is a wasting asset that will eventually need to be demolished and replaced, say, in 60 or 80 years, but not in the life of a typical business plan. Depreciation expense, in the early years, is typically more than enough to offset the principal reduction portion of the mortgage payments, and to create excess tax write-off possibilities for the owner, which might well be your for-profit subsidiary. Accounting losses due to depreciation make it difficult for many investors in securities to understand the true value of shares of beneficial interest in publicly held Real Estate Investment Trusts.

Appreciation

At the same time as depreciation is being deducted, however, the property is normally increasing in value due to inflation, which is called appreciation. The property is not actually decreasing in value as would be expected in the case of business equipment, such as a vehicle or a computer. While $100,000 paid for cars will depreciate to almost zero in 15 years, $100,000 paid for well-located real estate could easily become worth close to $200,000 during the same 15-year period. Therefore, being able to depreciate the building for tax purposes becomes a wonderful tax advantage for taxpayers, such as your for-profit subsidiary that holds title to the income property.

While $100,000 paid for cars will depreciate to almost zero in 15 years, $100,000 paid for well-located real estate could easily become worth close to $200,000 during the same 15-year period.

Capitalization Rate

Net Operating Income is a necessary factor in determining capitalization rate. The capitalization rate equals the net operating income divided by the present value. For example, a capitalization rate of 10% would be determined by dividing a property's net operating income of $100,000 by its present value of $1 million.

$$10\% = \frac{\$100,000}{\$1,000,000}$$

Buffett's view in regard to return on invested capital

Warren Buffett would regularly tell his mangers to not be so concerned about growth in sales, or even profit as an isolated number, but rather, the return on invested capital is the most important indicator of successful management.

In the real estate marketplace, as in all investment risk reward ratios, high capitalization rates correlate, to a large degree, to more risk and more intensive management. As an example, an older apartment complex in just average condition, and a few less tenants, might be bought at a lower price, yielding a higher capitalization rate of say 11% or 12%, but requiring more hands-on management. On the other hand, a newer shopping center located in the path of progress and requiring less intensive management would be expected to sell at price with correspondingly lower capitalization rate, say 7.5% or 8.5%. As this was being written, the author received an offer to bid on a coffee shop net leased to Starbucks in Valdosta, Georgia, with a net operating income of $93,450 and an asking price of $1,500,000.00, indicating a capitalization rate of 6.25%. If a prospective buyer demanded a capitalization rate of 7%, his offer would therefore be only $1,335,000.

Freedom from management and freedom from down payment. What's not to like about that?

If you are a full time pastor, you may gladly accept a lower return, in order not to work so hard to achieve it. This could be a prudent choice for a hands-off non-profit organization without expertise to handle intensive management, especially when you are getting the whole down payment for free. Freedom from management and freedom from down payment: what's not to like about that?

"The loftier the building,
the deeper must the foundation be laid."

- Thomas A. Kempis, Christian theologian
and author. (1379-1471)

Chapter 13

PROPERTY DUE DILIGENCE

"The man who represents himself
has a fool for a client."
–Anon

Legal Counsel

WHY SHOULD YOU HIRE A LAWYER WHEN OTHER ADVI-
sors seem knowledgeable? The old saying "The man who
represents himself has a fool for a client." –Anon, is still as true
as ever. Also you do "get what you pay for." Lawyers have to
finish both undergraduate and law school, pass the bar, and
continue their legal education throughout their careers. The
field of charitable giving is extremely complicated and

nuanced; every case is different. Don't proceed without competent legal counsel.

Environmental Site Assessment

A Phase 1 environmental site assessment, also known as a due diligence ESA, accomplishes the following: It will ascertain if the property is in compliance with environmental regulations at the federal, state and local levels. Noncompliance issues will be pointed out. Solutions will be suggested to comply with regulations and reduce your exposure to environmental liability. A Phase 1 ESA consists of three parts:

(1) An examination of government records and interviews with government officials, about the Property and contiguous properties; (2) A site investigation of the property and all buildings thereon; and (3) A study of the resulting information and a written report of findings and recommendations.

For a small cost, the due diligence shown by completing a Phase 1 environmental site assessment can reduce exposure to environmental liability.

Physical Inspection of Property

A property inspection is a visual inspection of the structure and components of a building to find items that are not performing correctly or items that are unsafe. If a problem or a symptom of a problem is found, the inspector will include a description of the problem in a written report and may recommend further evaluation. A buyer needs an inspection to find out all the problems possible with the property before closing on the purchase.

Also, more and more sellers are choosing to have a thorough inspection before selling, so as to provide full disclosure.

By doing so, the seller has demonstrated that he did what he could do to reveal any defects within the property. Although most properties have some defect, invariably there is an answer. Sometimes it requires a repair and other times it requires reducing the sale price. The property inspection addresses the problem well before the closing. The inspection report reveals the condition of the heating system, central air conditioning system, plumbing and electrical systems; the roof, attic, walls, ceilings, floors, windows and doors; the foundation, and the basement.

Appraiser

Although it is the donor's responsibility to have the property appraised before his next return is due, Treasury Regulations section 301.6501(c)-1 requires the following information be disclosed on a return:

- A description of the transferred property and any consideration received by the transferor.

- The identity of, and relationship between, the transferor and each transferee.

- A detailed description of the method used to determine the fair market value of the property transferred, including any financial data used in determining the value of the interest.

- A statement describing any position taken that is contrary to any proposed, temporary, or final regulation, or revenue ruling, published at the time of the transfer.

The IRS requires that the appraiser must meet all of the following requirements:

- The appraiser holds out to the public as an appraiser or performs appraisals on a regular basis.

- The appraiser is qualified to make appraisals of the property being valued.
- The appraiser is not the donor or the donee of the property or a member of the family of the donor or donee [as defined in section 2032A (e)(2)], or any person employed by the donor, the donee, or a member of the family of either.

Further, Treasury Regulations section 301.6501(c)-1 requires that the appraisal contain all of the following:

- The date of the transfer, the date on which the transferred property was appraised, and the purpose of the appraisal.
- A description of the property.
- A description of the appraisal process employed.
- A description of the assumptions, hypothetical conditions, and any limiting conditions and restrictions of the transferred property that affect the analysis, opinions, and conclusions.
- The information considered in determining the appraised value, including, in the case of an ownership interest in a business, all financial data that was used in determining the value of the interest that is sufficiently detailed so that another person can replicate the process and arrive at the appraised value.
- The appraisal procedures followed, and the reasoning that supports the analysis, opinions, and conclusions.
- The valuation method being utilized, the rationale for the valuation method, and the procedure used in determining the fair market value of the asset transferred.
- The specific basis for the valuation, such as specific comparable sales or transactions, sales of similar inter-

ests, asset-based approaches, and merger-acquisitions transactions.

Architect

Skillfully blending art and science, your architectural firm will translate your space requirements into a plan for a structure that reflects your goals, bringing harmony between exterior and interior spaces, while respecting existing architectural elements.

In your due diligence phase, your architect, being knowledgeable in local zoning ordinances and building regulations, will assess the feasibility of your intended use. If rezoning is necessary, the architect will illustrate the facility on a site plan at the optimum location for your property and he will meet with you and the zoning officials to advance the rezoning process.

Select an architectural firm which has a broad experience in the design of your type of building. Inspect some completed facilities which the architectural firm has previously designed. Talk to former clients.

At this stage, it is important to have key members of your leadership team involved. Because form follows function, your leaders should express how they envision the facility could be utilized to meet their requirements. The more input at this stage, the better the resulting buildings will meet your needs on a long-term basis.

During the interview process, assess the degree of rapport you have established. You want to be confident of excellent communication over the long-term required to successfully complete such a large and important project where the impact is so far reaching. Finally, you and the architectural firm should execute a written contract covering all the terms of your agreement.

Realtors

The purchase of real estate is, for most people, the largest transaction they will ever consummate. The complexity, cost, and risk involved is daunting. In the early days of my real estate career the standard real estate purchase form approved by our local Board of Realtors and the Bar Association was all contained on the front and back of one page. In the current age of consumerism, various reports have become mandatory, including seller's disclosures, agency disclosures, environmental information and property inspection reports.

Realtors work with contracts daily, and can point out which real estate items are in your favor or not. Your Realtor can discuss with you the various elements of the property features and characteristics. He can provide guidance in the framing of a reasonable initial offer. Obviously, as the buyer, you want the lowest price; and seller wants the highest price. Your agent can assist you in the property details. Agents must (1) obey the principal's instructions (so long as they are within the law); (2) be loyal to the principal's interests; (3) act in good faith; (4) use professional judgment, skill, and ability in his/ her actions; (5) account for all money belonging to others that comes into their possession; (6) perform agency duties in person; and (7) keep the principal fully informed as to developments affecting their relationships. It is always recommended that each party be represented by legal counsel.

Ordinarily, you will not pay until closing for any services performed by a Realtor. Neither in advance, nor as the transaction progresses. The fee is only due if and when it closes. All the costs paid or incurred on your behalf are absorbed by the Realtor, and if there is no closing, he is not reimbursed. Not too many other professions will work on that basis. That is why your agent endeavors to effectively and purposefully get you to a successful closing.

> One of the greatest and most profitable advantages of buyer brokerage is that the buyer's Realtor will pursue the very finest acquisition opportunities, whether or not they are listed for sale on the market.

Realtor's fees are negotiable. You may be able to negotiate a lower fee if you want fewer services. But remember a basic axiom of business: "You can eliminate the middleman but you cannot eliminate the middleman's function." Just one slip-up on the buyer's part for what might seem to be a minor detail could easily offset the value of the entire fee, especially on a complicated commercial transaction. In the case of a commercial or nonprofit buyer, it is common for the Realtor to work under a buyer's brokerage agreement, which allows him to pursue acquiring the best property suited to your needs. The buyer's broker will keep the buyer's inside information and overall goals confidential. He will negotiate with the objective of obtaining the lowest price for the buyer. The buyer's broker will work to protect the buyer's best interests at all times.

One of the greatest and most profitable advantages of

buyer brokerage is that the buyer's Realtor will pursue the very finest acquisition opportunities, whether or not they are listed for sale on the market. Often you will hear that some prime real estate has transferred, even though no one knew it was for sale. The reason is that it was never listed for sale. The owner was approached directly by the Realtor who represented a buyer who was paying the brokerage fee. This method is used by the most savvy and wealthy property investors in the world. It really doesn't matter that you, as buyer, are paying the fee. If the contract says the seller is to pay the fee at closing, who really supplies all the money so the seller can pay the fee? The buyer. Sophisticated buyers and sellers realize that the fee merely makes up part of the purchase price, regardless of who pays it. What really matters is that you get the property you actually want, at the bargain sale price you want to pay.

Afterword

"Success in life or business is not fully represented by
land, business ownership, stocks and bonds, or cash.
In addition to earthly capital we need to add to our
store of intellectual and spiritual capital."

— Jon Hanson, author of *Good Debt, Bad
Debt: Knowing the Difference Can Save Your
Financial Life*

I HAVE BEEN LIGHT-HEARTEDLY TELLING MY WIFE,
Diane, after each of these transactions was closed: "This
transaction should be in the book that I will write some day.
Several of my long-time highly experienced commercial
investor clients in the for-profit world are looking full time
for investments that would yield these kinds of returns on
invested capital. How is it that church buyers obtain these
magnificent results, with virtually no investment training or
experience?

It was certainly not my expertise. But something miracu-
lous happens when you turn your hand to help those who help
others. This is the unearned increment not articulated by
either Karl Marx or Adam Smith. This is the immutable law
of the universe, for those who give, as unto the Lord: *"Give,
and it shall be given unto you. Good measure, pressed down, and
shaken together, and running over, shall men give into your
bosom."* — Luke 16:38 (KJV)

Be well; do good; place all your faith in Christ; and I'll see you There.

"In all thy ways, acknowledge Him,
and He will direct thy path."

-Solomon

Appendix A

IRS FORMS 8282 AND 8283

Form **8282**
(Rev. September 1998)
Department of the Treasury
Internal Revenue Service

Donee Information Return
(Sale, Exchange, or Other Disposition of Donated Property)
► See instructions on back.

OMB No. 1545-0908

Give a Copy to Donor

Please Print or Type

Name of charitable organization (donee)

Address (number, street, and room or suite no.)

City or town, state, and ZIP code

Employer identification number

Part I — Information on ORIGINAL DONOR and DONEE Receiving the Property

1a Name(s) of the original donor of the property

1b Identifying number

Note: Complete lines 2a–2d only if you gave this property to another charitable organization (successor donee).

2a Name of charitable organization

2b Employer identification number

2c Address (number, street, and room or suite no.)

2d City or town, state, and ZIP code

Note: If you are the original donee, skip Part II and go to Part III now.

Part II — Information on PREVIOUS DONEES—Complete this part only if you were not the first donee to receive the property. If you were the second donee, leave lines 4a–4d blank. If you were a third or later donee, complete lines 3a–4d. On lines 4a–4d, give information on the preceding donee (the one who gave you the property).

3a Name of original donee

3b Employer identification number

3c Address (number, street, and room or suite no.)

3d City or town, state, and ZIP code

4a Name of preceding donee

4b Employer identification number

4c Address (number, street, and room or suite no.)

4d City or town, state, and ZIP code

Part III — Information on DONATED PROPERTY—If you are the original donee, leave column (c) blank.

(a) Description of donated property sold, exchanged, or otherwise disposed of (if you need more space, attach a separate statement)	(b) Date you received the item(s)	(c) Date the first donee received the item(s)	(d) Date item(s) sold, exchanged, or otherwise disposed of	(e) Amount received upon disposition

For Paperwork Reduction Act Notice, see back of form.

Cat. No. 62307Y

Form **8282** (Rev. 9-98)

General Instructions

Section references are to the Internal Revenue Code

Purpose of Form

Donee organizations use Form 8282 to report information to the IRS about dispositions of certain charitable deduction property made within 2 years after the donor contributed the property.

Definitions

Note: *For Form 8282 and these instructions, the term "donee" includes all donees, unless specific reference is made to "original" or "successor" donee.*

Original donee. The first donee to or for which the donor gave the property. The original donee is required to sign an Appraisal Summary presented by the donor for charitable deduction property.

Successor donee. Any donee of property other than the original donee.

Appraisal summary. Section B of Form 8283, Noncash Charitable Contributions.

Charitable deduction property. Property (other than money or certain publicly traded securities) for which the original donee signed, or was presented with for signature, the Appraisal Summary (Form 8283, Section B).

Generally, only items or groups of similar items for which the donor claimed a deduction of more than $5,000 are included on the Appraisal Summary. There is an exception if a donor gives similar items to more than one donee organization and the total deducted for these similar items exceeds $5,000. For example, if a donor deducts $2,000 for books given to a donee organization and $4,000 for books to another donee organization, the donor must present a separate Appraisal Summary to each organization. For more information, see the Instructions for Form 8283.

Who Must File

Original and successor donee organizations must file Form 8282 if they sell, exchange, consume, or otherwise dispose of (with or without consideration) charitable deduction property within 2 years after the date the original donee received the property. See **Charitable deduction property** earlier.

Exceptions. There are two situations where Form 8282 does not have to be filed.

1. *Items valued at $500 or less.* You do not have to file Form 8282 if, at the time the original donee signed the Appraisal Summary, the donor had signed a statement on Form 8283 that the appraised value of the specific item was not more than $500. If Form 8283 contains more than one similar item, this exception applies only to those items that are clearly identified as having a value of $500 or less. However, for purposes of the donor's

determination of whether the appraised value of the item exceeds $500, all shares of nonpublicly traded stock, or items that form a set, are considered one item. For example, a collection of books written by the same author, components of a stereo system, or six place settings of a pattern of silverware are considered one item.

2. *Items consumed or distributed for charitable purpose.* You do not have to file Form 8282 if an item is consumed or distributed, without consideration, in fulfilling your purpose or function as a tax exempt organization. For example, no reporting is required for medical supplies consumed or distributed by a tax-exempt relief organization in aiding disaster victims.

When To File

If you dispose of charitable deduction property within 2 years of the date the original donee received it and you do not meet exception **1** or **2** above, you must file Form 8282 within 125 days after the date of disposition.

Exception. If you did not file because you had no reason to believe the substantiation requirements applied to the donor, but you later become aware that they did apply, file Form 8282 within 60 days after the date you become aware you are liable. For example, this exception would apply where an Appraisal Summary is furnished to a successor donee after the date that donee disposes of the charitable deduction property.

Missing Information

If Form 8282 is filed by the due date, you must enter your organization's name, address, and EIN and complete at least Part III, column (i). You do not have to complete the remaining items if the information is not available. For example, you may not have the information necessary to complete all entries if the donor's Appraisal Summary is not available to you.

Where To File

Send Form 8282 to the Internal Revenue Service, Ogden, UT 84201-0027.

Penalty

You may be subject to a penalty if you fail to file this form by the due date, fail to include all of the information required to be shown on this form, or fail to include correct information on this form (see **Missing Information** above). The penalty is generally $50. For more details, see section 6721.

Other Requirements

Information you must give a successor donee. If the property is transferred to another charitable organization within the 2-year period discussed earlier, you must give your successor donee all of the following information:

1. The name, address, and EIN of your organization.

2. A copy of the Appraisal Summary (the Form 8283 that you received from the donor or a preceding donee).

3. A copy of this Form 8282 within 15 days after you file it.

You must furnish items **1** and **2** above within 15 days after the latest of the date:

• You transferred the property,

• The original donee signed the Appraisal Summary, or

• You received a copy of the Appraisal Summary from the preceding donee if you are also a successor donee.

Information the successor donee must give you. The successor donee organization to whom you transferred this property is required to give you their organization's name, address, and EIN within 15 days after the later of:

• The date you transferred the property, or

• The date they received a copy of the Appraisal Summary.

Information you must give the donor. You must give a copy of your Form 8282 to the original donor of the property.

Recordkeeping. You must keep a copy of the Appraisal Summary in your records.

Paperwork Reduction Act Notice. We ask for the information on this form to carry out the Internal Revenue laws of the United States. You are required to give us the information. We need it to ensure that you are complying with these laws and to allow us to figure and collect the right amount of tax.

You are not required to provide the information requested on a form that is subject to the Paperwork Reduction Act unless the form displays a valid OMB control number. Books or records relating to a form or its instructions must be retained as long as their contents may become material in the administration of any Internal Revenue law. Generally, tax returns and return information are confidential, as required by section 6103.

The time needed to complete this form will vary depending on individual circumstances. The estimated average time is:

Recordkeeping . . . . . . 3 hr., 7 min.

Learning about the law
or the form . . . . 35 min.

Preparing and sending
the form to the IRS . . . . . 41 min.

If you have comments concerning the accuracy of these time estimates or suggestions for making this form simpler, we would be happy to hear from you. You can write to the Tax Forms Committee, Western Area Distribution Center, Rancho Cordova, CA 95743-0001. **DO NOT** send the form to this address. Instead, see **Where To File** on this page.

Form **8283**

(Rev. December 2006)

Department of the Treasury
Internal Revenue Service

Noncash Charitable Contributions

► Attach to your tax return if you claimed a total deduction
of over $500 for all contributed property.

► See separate instructions.

OMB No. 1545-0908

Attachment
Sequence No. **155**

Name(s) shown on your income tax return | Identifying number

Note. Figure the amount of your contribution deduction before completing this form. See your tax return instructions.

Section A. Donated Property of $5,000 or Less and Certain Publicly Traded Securities—List in this section **only** items (or groups of similar items) for which you claimed a deduction of $5,000 or less. Also, list certain publicly traded securities even if the deduction is more than $5,000 (see instructions).

Part I **Information on Donated Property**—If you need more space, attach a statement.

1	(a) Name and address of the donee organization	(b) Description of donated property (For a donated vehicle, enter the year, make, model, condition, and mileage, and attach Form 1098-C if required.)
A		
B		
C		
D		
E		

Note. If the amount you claimed as a deduction for an item is $500 or less, you do not have to complete columns (d), (e), and (f).

	(c) Date of the contribution	(d) Date acquired by donor (mo., yr.)	(e) How acquired by donor	(f) Donor's cost or adjusted basis	(g) Fair market value (see instructions)	(h) Method used to determine the fair market value
A						
B						
C						
D						
E						

Part II **Partial Interests and Restricted Use Property**—Complete lines 2a through 2e if you gave less than an entire interest in a property listed in Part I. Complete lines 3a through 3c if conditions were placed on a contribution listed in Part I; also attach the required statement (see instructions).

2a Enter the letter from Part I that identifies the property for which you gave less than an entire interest ► _____ .
If Part II applies to more than one property, attach a separate statement.

b Total amount claimed as a deduction for the property listed in Part I: **(1)** For this tax year ► _____ .
(2) For any prior tax years ► _____ .

c Name and address of each organization to which any such contribution was made in a prior year (complete only if different from the donee organization above):

Name of charitable organization (donee)

Address (number, street, and room or suite no.)

City or town, state, and ZIP code

d For tangible property, enter the place where the property is located or kept ► _____

e Name of any person, other than the donee organization, having actual possession of the property ► _____

		Yes	No
3a	Is there a restriction, either temporary or permanent, on the donee's right to use or dispose of the donated property?		
b	Did you give to anyone (other than the donee organization or another organization participating with the donee organization in cooperative fundraising) the right to the income from the donated property or to the possession of the property, including the right to vote donated securities, to acquire the property by purchase or otherwise, or to designate the person having such income, possession, or right to acquire?		
c	Is there a restriction limiting the donated property for a particular use?		

For Paperwork Reduction Act Notice, see separate instructions.   Cat. No. 62299J   Form **8283** (Rev. 12-2006)

Form 8283 (Rev. 12-2006)   Page **2**

Name(s) shown on your income tax return   **Identifying number**

Section B. Donated Property Over $5,000 (Except Certain Publicly Traded Securities)—List in this section only items (or groups of similar items) for which you claimed a deduction of more than $5,000 per item or group (except contributions of certain publicly traded securities reported in Section A). An appraisal is generally required for property listed in Section B (see instructions).

Part I   **Information on Donated Property**—To be completed by the taxpayer and/or the appraiser.

4   Check the box that describes the type of property donated:

☐ Art* (contribution of $20,000 or more)   ☐ Qualified Conservation Contribution   ☐ Equipment
☐ Art* (contribution of less than $20,000)   ☐ Other Real Estate   ☐ Securities
☐ Collectibles**   ☐ Intellectual Property   ☐ Other

*Art includes paintings, sculptures, watercolors, prints, drawings, ceramics, antiques, decorative arts, textiles, carpets, silver, rare manuscripts, historical memorabilia, and other similar objects.
**Collectibles include coins, stamps, books, gems, jewelry, sports memorabilia, dolls, etc., but not art as defined above.

Note. In certain cases, you must attach a qualified appraisal of the property. See instructions.

5	(a) Description of donated property (if you need more space, attach a separate statement)	(b) If tangible property was donated, give a brief summary of the overall physical condition of the property at the time of the gift	(c) Appraised fair market value
A			
B			
C			
D			

	(d) Date acquired by donor (mo., yr.)	(e) How acquired by donor	(f) Donor's cost or adjusted basis	(g) For bargain sales, enter amount received	See instructions	
					(h) Amount claimed as a deduction	(i) Average trading price of securities
A						
B						
C						
D						

Part II   **Taxpayer (Donor) Statement**—List each item included in Part I above that the appraisal identifies as having a value of $500 or less. See instructions.

I declare that the following item(s) included in Part I above has to the best of my knowledge and belief an appraised value of not more than $500 (per item). Enter identifying letter from Part I and describe the specific item. See instructions. ▶ _____

Signature of taxpayer (donor) ▶   Date ▶

Part III   **Declaration of Appraiser**

I declare that I am not the donor, the donee, a party to the transaction in which the donor acquired the property, employed by, or related to any of the foregoing persons, or married to any person who is related to any of the foregoing persons. And, if regularly used by the donor, donee, or party to the transaction, I performed the majority of my appraisals during my tax year for other persons.

Also, I declare that I hold myself out to the public as an appraiser or perform appraisals on a regular basis; and that because of my qualifications as described in the appraisal, I am qualified to make appraisals of the type of property being valued. I certify that the appraisal fees were not based on a percentage of the appraised property value. Furthermore, I understand that a false or fraudulent overstatement of the property value as described in the qualified appraisal or this Form 8283 may subject me to the penalty under section 6701(a) (aiding and abetting the understatement of tax liability). In addition, I understand that a substantial or gross valuation misstatement resulting from the appraisal of the value of the property that I know, or reasonably should know, would be used in connection with a return or claim for refund, may subject me to the penalty under section 6695A. I affirm that I have not been barred from presenting evidence or testimony by the Office of Professional Responsibility.

Sign
Here   Signature ▶   Title ▶   Date ▶

Business address (including room or suite no.)   **Identifying number**

City or town, state, and ZIP code

Part IV   **Donee Acknowledgment**—To be completed by the charitable organization.

This charitable organization acknowledges that it is a qualified organization under section 170(c) and that it received the donated property as described in Section B, Part I, above on the following date ▶ _____

Furthermore, this organization affirms that in the event it sells, exchanges, or otherwise disposes of the property described in Section B, Part I (or any portion thereof) within 3 years after the date of receipt, it will file **Form 8282**, Donee Information Return, with the IRS and give the donor a copy of that form. This acknowledgment does not represent agreement with the claimed fair market value.

Does the organization intend to use the property for an unrelated use? . . . . ▶ ☐ Yes ☐ No

Name of charitable organization (donee)   Employer identification number

Address (number, street, and room or suite no.)   City or town, state, and ZIP code

Authorized signature   Title   Date

Printed on Recycled Paper   Form **8283** (Rev. 12-2006)

Appendix B

TREASURY REGULATIONS

TREASURY REGULATIONS SECTION 301.6501(C)-1 requires the following information be disclosed on a return:

- A description of the transferred property and any consideration received by the transferor.

- The identity of, and relationship between, the transferor and each transferee.

- A detailed description of the method used to determine the fair market value of the property transferred, including any financial data used in determining the value of the interest.

- A statement describing any position taken that is contrary to any proposed, temporary, or final regulation, or revenue ruling, published at the time of the transfer.

The IRS requires that the appraiser must meet all of the following requirements:

- The appraiser holds out to the public as an appraiser or performs appraisals on a regular basis.

- The appraiser is qualified to make appraisals of the property being valued.

- The appraiser is not the donor or the donee of the property or a member of the family of the donor or

donee [as defined in section 2032A (e)(2)], or any
person employed by the donor, the donee, or a
member of the family of either.

Further, Treasury Regulations section 301.6501(c)-1
requires that the appraisal contain all of the following:

- The date of the transfer, the date on which the transferred property was appraised, and the purpose of the
  appraisal.
- A description of the property.
- A description of the appraisal process employed.
- A description of the assumptions, hypothetical conditions, and any limiting conditions and restrictions of
  the transferred property that affect the analysis, opinions, and conclusions.
- The information considered in determining the
  appraised value, including, in the case of an ownership
  interest in a business, all financial data that was used
  in determining the value of the interest that is sufficiently detailed so that another person can replicate
  the process and arrive at the appraised value.
- The appraisal procedures followed, and the reasoning
  that supports the analysis, opinions, and conclusions.
- The valuation method being utilized, the rationale for
  the valuation method, and the procedure used in
  determining the fair market value of the asset transferred.
- The specific basis for the valuation, such as specific
  comparable sales or transactions, sales of similar interests, asset-based approaches, and merger-acquisitions
  transactions.

Appendix C

IRS Life Expectancy Table

Publication 590,
Appendix C, Pages 79, 80

APPENDIX C. Life Expectancy Tables

Table I
(Single Life Expectancy)
(For Use by Beneficiaries)

Age	Life Expectancy	Age	Life Expectancy
0	82.4	28	55.3
1	81.6	29	54.3
2	80.6	30	53.3
3	79.7	31	52.4
4	78.7	32	51.4
5	77.7	33	50.4
6	76.7	34	49.4
7	75.8	35	48.5
8	74.8	36	47.5
9	73.8	37	46.5
10	72.8	38	45.6
11	71.8	39	44.6
12	70.8	40	43.6
13	69.9	41	42.7
14	68.9	42	41.7
15	67.9	43	40.7
16	66.9	44	39.8
17	66.0	45	38.8
18	65.0	46	37.9
19	64.0	47	37.0
20	63.0	48	36.0
21	62.1	49	35.1
22	61.1	50	34.2
23	60.1	51	33.3
24	59.1	52	32.3
25	58.2	53	31.4
26	57.2	54	30.5
27	56.2	55	29.6

APPENDIX C. (Continued)

Table I
(Single Life Expectancy)
(For Use by Beneficiaries)

Age	Life Expectancy	Age	Life Expectancy
56	28.7	84	8.1
57	27.9	85	7.6
58	27.0	86	7.1
59	26.1	87	6.7
60	25.2	88	6.3
61	24.4	89	5.9
62	23.5	90	5.5
63	22.7	91	5.2
64	21.8	92	4.9
65	21.0	93	4.6
66	20.2	94	4.3
67	19.4	95	4.1
68	18.6	96	3.8
69	17.8	97	3.6
70	17.0	98	3.4
71	16.3	99	3.1
72	15.5	100	2.9
73	14.8	101	2.7
74	14.1	102	2.5
75	13.4	103	2.3
76	12.7	104	2.1
77	12.1	105	1.9
78	11.4	106	1.7
79	10.8	107	1.5
80	10.2	108	1.4
81	9.7	109	1.2
82	9.1	110	1.1
83	8.6	111 and over	1.0

Glossary

Acceleration Clause A clause in a mortgage or note providing the lender with the option to declare the entire outstanding balance immediately due and payable in the event of default

Acceptance of Deed The taking of the deed physically by the grantee

Acceptance of Offer The purchaser's or seller's agreement to the terms offered by the other party

Accrued Interest Deferred interest which has been earned, but with payment deferred

Acknowledgement A declaration before a notary public of one's signing of an instrument

Adjustable Rate Mortgage Loan A loan with an adjustable interest rate as determined by changes in a selected index

Agreement of Sale Contract executed by purchaser and seller containing the terms, conditions and provisions of sale under which a property is to be sold

Amortized Mortgage A mortgage requiring periodic payments which will repay the entire loan by the end of the loan term

Appraisal A written estimate of market value prepared by an individual who is unbiased and knowledgeable

Assignment The Assignor's conveyance of right, title and ownership in property to an Assignee

Assumption A method of acquiring real estate in which the purchaser agrees to become liable for repaying the existing mortgage indebtedness

Balloon Mortgage A mortgage loan with periodic payments for a number of years ending with one large final payment for the unpaid balance, referred to as the balloon payment

Blanket Mortgage A mortgage that covers two or more properties

Broker A person who brings purchasers and sellers together and helps to negotiate the purchase agreement

Closing The consummation of a real estate transaction when legal documents are executed and funds are disbursed for the purchase or financing of the property; also referred to as the Settlement

Collateral Assets hypothecated as security for a loan

Commission Compensation paid to a real estate broker for bringing purchaser and seller together and negotiating a real estate transaction

Contingency A condition to be satisfied before the parties are legally bound to consummate an agreement

Contract of Sale The written agreement between the purchaser and seller setting forth the price and terms of sale

Conventional Loan A loan not guaranteed or insured by the government

Deed The instrument by which title to real estate is conveyed from grantor to grantee. It contains a legal description of the property. It is signed, witnessed, notarized and delivered to the purchaser at settlement

Default Failure to meet the terms of a contract, including nonpayment

Delinquency Failure to make payments on time as agreed in the note

Discount Points An upfront fee paid by the borrower to the lender at settlement. One point equals 1% of the total loan amount. Interest rates and points or inversely related, i.e. the less points you pay the higher your interest rate.

Down Payment The amount of the purchase price paid at the closing by purchaser in cash

Due-on-Sale Clause Mortgage clause permitting the lender, at its option, to demand immediate payment in full in the event property is sold or transferred in any manner

Earnest Money Good-faith deposit paid by the purchaser, usually to the broker, toward the purchase price at signing of the purchase agreement

General Warranty Deed A deed conveying real estate containing a covenant that the grantor will warrant and defend the title as to all claims

Grace Period A period of time specified in the loan agreement during which a loan payment may be paid after the date due, without incurring a late charge

Grantee Person who receives from the grantor a deed for real estate

Grantor One who transfers real estate by deed

Gross Income Total income before deduction of any expenses

Hazard Insurance Insures the owner and the lender against losses arising from fire and other perils such as rain, explosion, vandalism, snow, hail, aircraft and windstorm. The policy owner pays to the insurance company a premium for the coverage either directly or through an impound account with the lender

Impound Account Escrow account held by the lender into which the borrower pays monthly installments, in addition to the payment for principal and interest, to cover annual expenses such as taxes and insurance

Index A published rate used to determine interest rate changes on the loan

Interest Amount payable for borrowing money expressed as a percentage of the remaining balance

Interest Rate The annual rate of interest on a note, calculated as a percentage

Joint Liability Obligation owed by two or more people, who are each liable for the entire amount

Joint Tenancy A form of group ownership vesting an equal interest in the property to each individual, and with rights of survivorship

Junior Mortgage A mortgage subject to the priority of a senior mortgage or lien. In the event of foreclosure the senior creditor is paid first.

Late Charge A fee incurred by a borrower as a penalty when the payment is not paid when due

Legal Description Written identification of the exact boundaries of the land. The legal description is included in or attached to the deed and or mortgage.

Lender The mortgage company, bank or other person providing the loan

Loan Application The borrower's statement of personal and financial information

Loan Application Fee Cost to borrower for loan processing costs, such as the credit report, appraisal fee and other costs incurred

Loan to Value Ratio (LTV) Ratio expressed as a percentage, calculated by dividing the amount borrowed by the lesser of the purchase price or the fair market value determined by an appraisal

Mortgage Document executed by the mortgagor and the delivered to the mortgagee pledging property as security for payment of amounts due under the mortgage note

Mortgage Banker The originator and/or servicer of the mortgage loan

Mortgage Broker A person who facilitates and processes mortgage financing for borrowers

Mortgage Loan A loan collateralized by real property

Mortgage Note Instrument executed by a borrower promising to repay the loan together with interest on certain dates, secured by a mortgage on real estate.

Mortgagee The mortgage loan lender.

Mortgagor The mortgage loan borrower

Note Instrument obligating a borrower to repay a loan at a specified interest rate at a certain time

Per Diem Interest Interest calculated on a daily basis

Power of Attorney Written authorization for one person to act on behalf of another person

Pre-Approval Ascertaining how much a perspective borrower may be able to finance, prior to application, with a preliminary review of a borrower's credit and an analysis of the income and expenses

Prepaid Interest Interest charged to borrower at time of settlement to cover the period until the due date of the first loan payment

Prepayment Full or partial repayment of the principal before the date provided in the note

Principal The outstanding balance of the debt, not counting interest, remaining due on the note

Purchase Agreement Contract between purchaser and seller setting forth the price, terms and conditions of the sale

Quit Claim Deed A deed operating as a release, conveying the title, interest or claim, if any, which the grantor may have in the real estate, without warranty of the title's validity

Real Estate The land and anything permanently attached to the land. Also sometimes referred to as real property

Real Property See *Real Estate*

Recording The act of filing a legal instrument such as a deed or mortgage with the appropriate government registry

Refinancing The process of paying off an existing mortgage note with the proceeds obtained from a new mortgage secured by the same real estate

Second Mortgage A subsequent mortgage placed on a property that ranks in priority junior to the existing first mortgage

Settlement See *Closing*

Settlement Statement A statement detailing the disbursements at closing of the purchase or refinancing real estate

Specific Performance Requiring a party to perform exactly as agreed under the precise terms of an agreement

Tax Impound See *Impound Account*

Tax Lien A claim in favor of a state or local government against a property for nonpayment of taxes

Tax Sale Sale of real estate by a government authority for nonpayment of taxes

Term The period of time between commencement of the loan and when the loan is due at maturity

Title Written evidence of rights of ownership and possession of real estate

Title Company A company that issues a policy insuring the title to the real estate

Title Insurance An insurance policy insuring against loss arising from claims over ownership

Title Search Examination of the public records to determine if the seller is the legal owner of the real estate and whether there are defects in the title

Transfer Tax Tax imposed when title passes to a new owner

Variable Rate Interest rate that may be adjusted upward or downward in response to money market fluctuations

Variance Government permission to improve or develop a property in a way not authorized by the existing zoning ordinance, due to a unique hardship

Verification of Deposit (VOD) Written verification by the borrower's financial institution as to the applicant's account balance and history

Verification of Employment (VOE) Written verification by the employer as to applicant's position and salary

Waiver Intentional relinquishment or surrender of some right, privilege or contingency

Suggested Reading

Books

The Artful Journey: Cultivating and Soliciting the Major Gift, by William T. Sturtevant, (Bonus Books, November 1, 1997)

Bruce R. Hopkins, Attorney, is the author of 11 books. They are:

The Law of Tax-Exempt Organizations (7th ed. 1998; annually supplemented) (8th edition is in progress).

The Tax Law of Charitable Giving (2nd ed. 2000; annually supplemented)

The Law of Fundraising (3rd ed. 2002; annually supplemented)

The Nonprofits' Guide to Internet Communications Law (October 2002)

Starting and Managing a Nonprofit Organization: A Legal Guide (3rd ed. 2001)

The Legal Answer Book for Nonprofit Organizations (1996)

The Second Legal Answer Book for Nonprofit Organizations (1999)

The First Legal Answer Book for Fund-Raisers (2000)

The Second Legal Answer Book for Fund-Raisers (2000)

The Nonprofit Law Dictionary (1994)

The Law of Intermediate Sanctions (Spring 2003

"UBIT Problems for Tax-Exempt Charitable Trusts," speech by Celia Roady, (for the Southern Federal Tax Institute, 35th Annual Institute, Atlanta, Georgia, September 21, 2000)

Tested Ways to Successful Fund Raising, by George A. Brakely (New York: AMACOM, A division of American Management Associations, 1980)

Successful Fundraising, A Complete Handbook for Volunteers and Professionals, by Joan Flanagan, (New York: Contemporary Books, 1991)

Joint ventures Involving Tax-Exempt Organizations, Second Edition by Michael I. Sanders (New York: John Wiley & Sons, Inc., 2000)

Bibliography

Barna. *How to Increase Giving in Your Church* (Ventura, California: Regal Books, 1997), p 13.

Bigelow, Bruce E. "Gifts of Real Estate." Article posted Wednesday, January 20, 1999 at 1:36 PM EST. The Planned Giving Design Center, www.pgdc.com/osu 19 April 2005 <http://www.pgdc.com/osu/item/?itemID=23747&bbp.i=8v n42o&gl1n.enc=ISO-8859-1>.

Brakely, George A. *Tested Ways to Successful Fund Raising*, New York: AMACOM, A division of American Management Associations, New York, 1980, p 26.

Buffett, Warren. 1997 speech at Caltech.

Busby, Don. *The Zondervan Church and Nonprofit Organization Tax and Financial Guide 2001 edition*, Grand Rapids, Michigan: Zondervan Publishing House, a division of Harper Collins Publishers), p35.

Flanagan, Joan. *Successful Fundraising, A Complete Handbook for Volunteers and Professionals*, (New York: Contemporary Books, 1991), p. 87.

Hurwit. Legal Perspectives for Nonprofit Managers, article on website, citing IRC § 514 (b)(3): Hurwit & Associates, Legal counsel for philanthropy and nonprofit sector, 4 April 2005 <http://www.hurwitassociates.com/l_21_managers. html>.

IRS Forms 8282 and 8283.

IRS Life Expectancy Table (2 pages), Publication 590: Appendix C, P79, 80.

IRS Publication 598 (Rev. March 2005), p 18.

IRS Revenue Ruling: (Rev. Rul. 81-163; 1981-1 C.B. 433).

Roady, Celia. *UBIT Problems for Tax-Exempt Charitable Trusts*, (Atlanta, Georgia: Speech given at the Southern Federal Tax Institute, 35th Annual Institute September 21, 2000, Atlanta, Georgia, Morgan, Lewis & Bockius LLP. 12 April, 2005

<http://www.morganlewis.com/pubs/A353BFFF-AA44-4FF3-AAE3C25E55A48AC3_Publication.pdf>.

Resources

Associations
Planned Giving Design Center is a national network of hosting organizations that proudly provide over 23,000 members with timely, objective content on the subjects of charitable taxation and planned giving; an engaging community; and a collection of services aimed at facilitating charitable gifts: www.Pgdc.com/usa

Attorneys
Bruce R. Hopkins, Attorney
Polsinelli Shalton & Welte PC
Kansas City, MO
(816) 753-1000
www.pswslaw.com

William Lane, Attorney
Lane, Alton & Horst
Columbus, Ohio
(614) 228-6885
www.lah4law.com

Celia Roady, Attorney
Morgan Lewis Counselors at Law
Washington DC
(202) 739-5279
www.morganlewis.com

Dirken Voelker, Attorney
Columbus, OH 43212
(614) 481-6500

Consultants
Roger Walker
Walker Consulting LLC
907 Riva Ridge Boulevard
Gahanna, OH 43230
(614) 519-5412

Online
(a) GuideStar — www.guidestar.org
The National Database of Nonprofit Organizations
Free service with information on the programs and finances
of more than 600,000 American charities and nonprofit
organizations.

(b) Giftlaw — www.Giftlaw.com
GiftLaw positions your organization for long-term relationships with financial advisors. With GiftLaw you will provide
ongoing education and encouragement to advisors toward
philanthropy.

(c) We Care America — www.WeCareAmerica.org
Local, regional and national faith-based and community ini-
tiatives

(d) The Foundation Center —- www.fountaioncenter.org

Index

501(C)(3) 59, 98, 100, 112

Abraham, Dan 37
acquisition indebtedness 98, 103
Akomeah, Bismark 44, 46
American Council on Gift Annuities 60, 63
appreciation 113

bargain sale 4-5, 37-39, 49-50, 52-53, 63, 92, 94, 98, 104-105, 107, 124
Bentley, Don 20, 36
Bigelow. Bruce E. 63
Bliss College 24-25, 27-28
Blue Cross Insurance Company 24-25
Bonhoeffer, Dietrich 57
Bowen, Barbara 42, 44
Boyd, Martin 42-43
Burkett, Larry 96
Busby, Daniel D. 99

Cameron, Mark 41
Capital City Church 24, 27-29
capital gains 50, 61, 104
capitalization rate 52, 114-115
Center of Vocational Alternatives (COVA) 27-28
Charitable Gift Annuity(ies) 59-64

Churchill, Winston Sir 22, 83
Columbus Real Estate Exchangers 4, 17, 26, 149
Cordle, Don xv
COVA 27-28
Crescendo 61, 64
Crosby, Fannie 88

debt 51-53, 92, 99, 103-105, 112
debt encumbered real estate 105
depreciation 51 102, 104, 112-113
donative intent 38, 50, 85, 93-94, 105
due diligence 7, 18, 44, 117-118, 121
Duncan, Travis 38

environmental site assessment 7, 118
Evangel Temple Assembly of God 35,37

Felty, Mel 44-45
Flanagan, Joan 142-143
Form 8282 56, 98, 127-128
Form 8283 56, 97-98, 129-130
for-profit subsidiary 100, 113

giftlaw 146

Glunt, David J. xv
Graham, Billy Rev. 47
GuideStar 146

Hanson, Jon xv, 51, 125
Hopkins, Bruce R. 141, 145
Hrabcak, Greg 27, 29
Hrabcak, Scott 27, 29

Internal Revenue Code 4-5,
    39, 49, 53, 85, 95, 106
Internal Revenue Service
    (IRS) 56, 61, 93, 95, 97-
    100, 102-103, 106, 119,
    131, 133

Jesus Power Assembly of God
    44-45

Kempis, Thomas A. 116

Lane, William 145
life expectancy 60-61, 133
Lowry, Connie 27
Lowry, Ron 27

McKnight Group 29

Neighborhood Land
    Exception 99
net operating income 52,
    111-112, 114-115

Palmer, Jim 23-25, 27

Reagan, Ronald W. 30
real estate encumbered by
    debt, 105
resale 56, 97, 104
Roady, Celia 100, 142, 144-
    145

Sanders, Michael I. 142
Solomon 89, 126
Speich, Gene 35-36
Strong, Jim FCBA xv
Sturtevant, William T. 93,
    141

Tinon, Furman 4, 26, 28

UBIT 54, 98, 100, 142
Unrelated Business Income
    54
Unrelated Business Income
    Tax 54, 98

Wallace, Ethan xi, xiii
Washington, George 16
We Care America 146
Wesley, John 2

About the Author

JAMES B. WOOTTON holds a Bachelor of Science degree in Business Administration from the Finance Department of the College of Administrative Sciences at The Ohio State University. Since his graduation, he has pursued the study of economics with Harvard University Extension School of Cambridge, Massachusetts. He is a graduate of the Realtors Institute.

Mr. Wootton has served for more than 20 years as a board member of both The Kiwanis Club of German Village and Teen Challenge of Columbus.

Engaged in commercial real estate brokerage since 1973, Mr. Wootton has negotiated many church property transactions, including some of the largest in the State of Ohio. He was president of the Columbus Real Estate Exchangers in 1986 and rose to become president of the statewide Ohio Commercial Realtors Exchange Association in 1988.

Mr. Wootton is a member of the Columbus, Ohio, and National Associations of Realtors, Columbus Commercial Industrial Investment Realtors, Columbus Real Estate Exchangers, and the Ohio Commercial Realtors Exchange Association. He and his wife, Diane, reside near Columbus, Ohio.

How to Contact the Author

Jim Wootton provides full consulting services for selected businesses, associations, and nonprofit organizations. Requests for information about these services, as well as inquiries about his availability for speeches and seminars, should be directed to him at the address below. Readers of this book are also encouraged to contact the author with comments and ideas for future editions.

Jim Wootton
American Charter LLC
8405 Pulsar Place, Suite 157
Columbus, Ohio 43240
Phone (614) 468-0198
Fax: (614) 355-0186
Email: JBW1688@Gmail.com
Website: www.therealestategift.com